Frivolity

NO LIMITS

NO LIMITS

Edited by Costica Bradatan

The most important questions in life haunt us with a sense of boundlessness: there is no one right way to think about them or an exclusive place to look for answers. Philosophers and prophets, poets and scholars, scientists and artists—all are right in their quest for clarity and meaning. We care about these issues not simply in themselves but for ourselves—for us. To make sense of them is to understand who we are better. No Limits brings together creative thinkers who delight in the pleasure of intellectual hunting, wherever the hunt may take them and whatever critical boundaries they have to trample as they go. And in so doing they prove that such searching is not just rewarding but also transformative. There are no limits to knowledge and self-knowledge—just as there are none to self-fashioning.

Connection: How Technology Can Make Us Better Humans, Dan Turello
Marginality: Solidarity and the Fight for Social Change, Jin Y. Park
Contemplation: The Movements of the Soul, Kevin Hart
Rapture, Christopher Hamilton
Storythinking: The New Science of Narrative Intelligence, Angus Fletcher
Taste: A Book of Small Bites, Jehanne Dubrow
Self-Improvement: Technologies of the Soul in the Age of Artificial Intelligence, Mark Coeckelbergh
Inwardness: An Outsider's Guide, Jonardon Ganeri
Touch: Recovering Our Most Vital Sense, Richard Kearney
Aimlessness, Tom Lutz
Intervolution: Smart Bodies Smart Things, Mark C. Taylor

Frivolity

Jehanne Dubrow

A DEFENSE

Columbia University Press
New York

Columbia University Press
Publishers Since 1893
New York Chichester, West Sussex
cup.columbia.edu

Cataloging-in-Publication Data is available from
the Library of Congress.

ISBN 9780231216142 (hardback)
ISBN 9780231216159 (trade paperback)
ISBN 9780231566629 (epub)
ISBN 9780231561150 (PDF)

LCCN 2026024528

Printed and bound by CPI Group (UK) Ltd, Croydon, CR0 4YY

Cover design: Chang Jae Lee

GPSR Authorized Representative: Easy Access System Europe, Mustamäe tee 50, 10621 Tallinn, Estonia, gpsr.requests@easproject.com

Contents

Frivolity

1

It will be the Year of Perfect Skin, I told myself. I had arrived at my mid-forties, and the mirror suddenly gave me a face crosshatched with creases. I was Portrait of a Woman Aging. I was a cubist composition, something by Picasso. I was a strange collage of exhaustion. Mouth, eyes, along the Cupid's bow of my lips—each one was crinkled like a piece of paper that had been balled up and then pressed flat again.

I no longer looked twenty years younger. But, worse, my skin had broken out in a strange midlife puberty. Every morning, another pink spot on my cheek. Every night, another small mark of embarrassment written along my jaw.

To begin the Year of Perfect Skin, I ordered creams and moisturizers, serums that arrived in glass ampules, oils I would measure out by the droplet. I learned to double-cleanse: first a balm that melted like butter, then a soapy liquid to wash all residue away. I ordered little disposable face towels from a company called Clean Skin Club, because immaculate skin was a society I wanted to join. I tapped something called essence into the fat of my cheekbones. My fingertips moved across my face the way they did across the keyboard of my laptop. I wanted glass skin, bouncy skin, skin slickened like the trail a snail leaves behind. Tap. Tap. I am revising myself, I said.

It was January 2020. Soon there would be a global pandemic. I would learn how to distance socially. I wore a disposable mask to the grocery store and a pair of surgical gloves. Standing in the produce section among the bins of apples, I grasped each piece of fruit with my blue, latex hand. Beneath the protective layers, I could smell the fear in my sweat.

Back home, I stood before the mirror's metallic scrutiny. Sometimes the mask left a welt around the perimeter of my mouth, a groove that briefly obscured my aging and acne.

What could I do in that year but insist on skin without flaws? What power did I have beyond leaning toward my own reflection and studying the lunar contours of a pore? If I stood close enough to the mirror, the world was reduced to my face. My skin became a whole topography. There was nothing beyond the landforms of forehead, nose, and chin.

2

Frivolity, meaning connected to the frivolous.[1] That is, unimportant, undeserving of rigorous thought.[2]

3

Frivolity is always intended as an insult. We deem certain lawsuits frivolous. Some entertainments. Some conversations. Frivolity is seldom a compliment we pay.

4

The word *frivolity* wears a feathered boa. When uttered, it is coquettish. It opens with an unvoiced *f*. It closes with what grammarians call a feminine ending, which seems to fizz like a pale splash of prosecco.

5

Feminine, because frivolity is stitched to gender. It is often tied to queerness and to color as well. Those who call an object "frivolous" criticize the thing and, by extension, they also critique the person who loves the snippet of lace, the leather fringe down the length of a sleeve.

6

Feminine, because items deemed frivolous—let's say a lipstick shaped like a sleek, red bullet of seduction—are mostly marketed and sold to women. Men's passions are taken seriously. The games they play as children become their weekend hobbies as adults, even if now they only watch a ball being hurled back and forth from the marshmallow cushions of their living rooms. Men are permitted to be fans. They can wear jerseys that hang to their knees, baggy shirts in primary colors, without censure. And *the game* (whatever that game might be) is never a frivolity.

But a woman who buys a bottle of perfume must be condemned for spending money on a silly spritz of mimosa and patchouli. She is judged for wanting *what women want*. Purses and heels. A dress made of something silky called charmeuse, a French word that means a woman who charms, one who bewitches.

And never mind that she has bought only what the market is selling. Never mind that she will be disparaged if her lips remain plain or her lashes lack the necessary coat of mascara, that caterpillar thickness. She should still be blamed for giving in to the allure of billboards ten feet tall with languorous models. Shame on her for wanting those vast cheekbones highlighted in gold, those great eyelids heavy with shadow the color of smoke.[3]

7

In *Ways of Seeing*, the art critic and writer John Berger examines the unkindness with which women are often viewed. The book considers the work of European artists, from the Middle Ages to the Renaissance and into the twentieth century. Berger examines the moral judgments that are embedded in representations of women's bodies, their lovely faces:

> The mirror was often used as a symbol of the vanity of woman. The moralizing, however, was mostly hypocritical.

> You painted a naked woman because you enjoyed looking at her, you put a mirror in her hand and you called the painting *Vanity*, thus morally condemning the woman whose nakedness you had depicted for your own pleasure.
>
> The real function of the mirror was otherwise. It was to make a woman connive in treating herself as, first and foremost, a sight.[4]

Berger shows us Hans Memling's *Vanity*. The piece is oil on wood. Created around 1485, it's one third of a triptych. A woman stands naked, except for her sandals and the thin, gold circlet in her hair. She holds a mirror. The only thing reflected is her face staring back from the glass. Although she's positioned in a landscape dense with greenery, dogs, a thatched cottage in the distance, she sees nothing but herself. We are meant to hate her for the way she has fallen into her own reflection. But why should she not? Her breasts are pert. Her belly's curve implies fecundity. A cloud of auburn hair hangs past her waist, reaching almost mid-thigh. Her flesh is so pale she might as well be alabaster, carved and polished smooth.

8

In Georges de La Tour's *The Penitent Magdalen*, the artist gives us another version of a woman. Painted circa 1640, she too sits before a mirror, this one rectangular, a frame placed within the frame of the painting. A gleaming skull is cushioned in her lap. Eyeless, it seems to gaze upward toward a candle that burns on the tabletop, the flame high and pale, voluptuous in its flickering, its image reflected in the glass.

As is typical of La Tour, the scene is split between brown shadow and stretches of brightness. The woman's face glows with light. The V of her white blouse plunges almost to her navel but not immodestly. She has none of the seductive vanity of Memling's subject. This must be Mary Magdalen reformed and healed, after her encounter with Christ. Although her skirt simmers red, some kind of heavy satin, she isn't presented as a figure of sexual pleasure. Her purity neuters her. Memento mori, such paintings instruct us: *Remember death.* Magdalen confronts herself in the mirror, neither delighting in her own beauty nor regretting its imminent loss. She is appropriately humble (as the artist sees it). Her self-regard is forgiven because she confronts her flaws. She acknowledges the corruption of skin.

9

Early on in George Eliot's great novel *Middlemarch,* Dorothea Brooke agrees to her younger sister's request that they finally divide between them their dead mother's jewelry. Dorothea is serious, pious, and beautiful. She wants not only to be a good Christian but also to appear like one to others. She wants to be seen as fastidiously unadorned, dressed only in her devotion to God. But the jewelry box holds some very pretty stuff, including "a necklace of purple amethysts set in exquisite gold work, and a pearl cross with five brilliants in it." Although she is tempted, Dorothea gives the piece to her sister, Celia. "A cross is the last thing I would wear as a trinket," she intones.[5]

A few paragraphs later, the girls discover an emerald and diamond ring. Dorothea is captivated by its sparkle and hue. "I suppose this is the reason why gems are used as spiritual emblems in the Revelation of St John," she muses. "They look like fragments of heaven. I think that emerald is more beautiful than any of them."[6] There is a matching bracelet, and Dorothea can't resist it either. She decides to keep the two pieces, although the ornaments require that she "justify her delight in the colours by merging them in her mystic religious joy." Celia notices her sister's philosophical inconsistencies and asks if Dorothea will wear the jewelry around other people. It's a moment of unusual tension between them, the biddable younger girl gently pointing out the elder's hypocrisy.

We are supposed to love Dorothea. She stands at the center of the narrative. But Eliot wants us to understand too how the young woman will suffer for her performances of virtue. She will marry someone older—Casaubon, a fussy and self-centered clergyman—who makes her miserable, all because she believes him to be a scholar and imagines a romantic life in which she might help him pursue academic distinction, the couple bent over the yellowed pages of books and parsing dense passages together.

In an essay titled "It Can Be Embarrassing to Love Dorothea," the novelist Pamela Erens reminds us:

> Eliot makes it clear that Dorothea is no saint but rather a morally immature young woman. Her self-denials have roots in youthful arrogance and impetuousness. . . . Dorothea doesn't recognize her bossiness and grandiosity. Her ideals of Christian humility and simplicity and service are genuine. But she is very young.[7]

Instead of admiring her mother's jewels for the sake of their splendor, the girl must rationalize her love for faceted stones. The gems glitter with holiness, she assures herself, because she cannot yet accept frivolous beauties on their own terms. Eliot departs here from the moralizing messages of Memling and La Tour. As the novelist sees it, ornamentation is not vanity. Dorothea's abnegation is.

10

The great Renaissance essayist Michel de Montaigne begins "Of Vanity" by arguing that there's nothing vainer than to write about vanity itself. "What the Divinity has so divinely told us about it ought to be carefully and continually meditated by people of understanding."[8] Montaigne is alluding to Ecclesiastes 1:2. "Vanity of vanities, saith the Preacher, vanity of vanities; all is vanity." In the Christian tradition, these words are a grim warning of our transience, the vaporous substance of our lives. To be distracted by vanities (read: frivolities) is to forget that earthly pleasures have no lasting value. They are temporary dust. The body is a candle that glimmers briefly. Only the soul persists.

But because Montaigne is subversive and a wit, he then devotes many pages to examining vanities, both his own and those of others. "Of Vanity" is as much a meditation on the experience of being a writer as it is a discussion of different forms of political rule. Then, just as it seems he has lost track of where he began, Montaigne returns to examining the matter:

> This common attitude and habit of looking elsewhere than at ourselves has been very useful for our own business. We are an object that fills us with discontent; we see nothing in us but misery and vanity. In order not to dishearten us, Nature has very appropriately thrown the action of our vision outward. We go forward with the current, but to turn our course back toward ourselves is a painful movement: thus the sea grows troubled and turbulent when it is tossed back on itself. Look, says everyone, at the movement of the heavens, look at the public, look at that man's quarrel, at this man's pulse, at another man's will; in short, always look high or low, or to one side, or in front, or behind you.[9]

We're all implicated in what Montaigne says. Vanity is what's false or empty. Vanity is the fruitless. We share in Montaigne's metaphor of the sea and feel uneasy when we are forced to encounter ourselves in the blue waves of self-reflection. We will do anything to avoid such crashing, drowning scrutiny. And this is where frivolity enters. The frivolous is a splendid excuse. It allows us to partake instead in the fun of gossip, to enjoy the delights of fashion and fragrance, to devour sugary cookies until our gluttony is sated, the soul fat as a full belly.

11

Often, Montaigne's writing has been seen as something of a frivolity in itself. Wide-ranging, funny, concerned equally with the public and the private, the grand and the small, his essays may perplex readers. Montaigne, after all, invented a new genre. Using himself as the subject matter, he created something unruly that is neither literature nor philosophy. Or, perhaps, he crafted a form that unites the two.

The essay, as its name tells us, attempts. It endeavors. It tries. Such an uncertain approach seems in opposition to the methodical work of philosophy. The philosopher defines terms, asks barbed questions, deduces, and eventually arrives at a rational conclusion. It might also seem foreign to the work of literature; the poet and the novelist set out to build a world from sensation and image, their language highly figured.

Literary scholar Victor Brombert offers a perfect summary of Montaigne's vision of the essay and its subjects, many of which might seem frivolous to an austere reader:

> No detail about his own person seems insignificant to him or undeserving to be written about: his physical appearance, his speech defects and way of walk, his digestive problems, his sleeping habits, the kidney stones that caused him so much pain, his taste in food and wines. He knows himself, or believes he does. For he also discovers himself and to a certain extent invents himself as he writes. The self he tries to describe remains in motion and not always easy to capture.[10]

Montaigne's invention is filled with doubt. Implicit in an essay is the chance of failure. The essayist tracks his own fidgety mind across long paragraphs. Readers follow this path of thought—out of pleasure and curiosity—not knowing where we are going or if we will ever arrive.

12

Montaigne in "We taste nothing pure" writes about the flaws of the human condition. He says we live in a state that makes it "impossible for things to come into our experience in their natural simplicity and purity."[11] Whatever we delight in "has an air of groaning and lament about it." And even the greatest joys have "more seriousness than gaiety." Later in the text, he observes that painters believe that the expressions formed by faces—their creases and wrinkles—must serve both for crying and for laughter.

If I am to follow Montaigne's argument, then I might say the frivolous is always tinged with solemnity, a gray pigment. The Year of Perfect Skin, for instance, was more than an example of self-centeredness, more than an effort to turn my face translucent, luminous as a moonstone set in silver prongs. It was my small way of insisting: *This body is alive and permanent.* The clearer my complexion became, the greater my distance from all the dying in that year.

13

In *Our Aesthetic Categories,* literary scholar Sianne Ngai analyzes the zany, the cute, and the interesting to explain how "aesthetic experience has been transformed by the hypercommodified, information-saturated, performance-driven conditions of late capitalism."[12] Each of these categories, she explains, is linked to a particular form of media as well as to certain genres of literature and forms of art. So, the zany is associated with comedy and "is hot: hot under the collar, hot and bothered, hot to trot."[13] The cute is connected to romance and can be seen as an "eroticization of powerlessness, evoking tenderness for 'small things' but also, sometimes, a desire to belittle or diminish them further."[14] And the interesting is related to realism. It "marks a tension between the unknown and the already known and is generally bound up with a desire to know and document reality," writes Ngai.[15]

Frivolity can be found in all three aesthetic categories. And perhaps this helps to explain why the frivolous is so often denigrated; frivolities are frequently viewed as the debris of late-stage capitalism. They are extravagances we pay too much for (with cash or, worse, credit). They are the entertainments on which we waste our time, the sensory experiences we can pursue only if we have wealth or privilege.

The flower-scented macaron is a cute frivolity. It's small enough to fit in the hand, a rounded pink shape made of egg white, sugar, crushed almonds, dried rose petals, and rosewater. The exclamation point—famously overused in contemporary communication—is a zany frivolity. It tries so hard to communicate playfulness and *fun!* all while doing the work of saying difficult, onerous things. The selfie and, in general, social media are interesting frivolities. The real is documented through photograph and word but curated, carefully filtered, made flawless for the sake of likes and followers.

14

It's easy to dismiss such matters. A critic of frivolities might say: *They represent our worst impulse to possess.* Gimme, gimme. But it takes skill to bake a cookie that tastes both of sweetened air and of a rose fresh-cut, still damp with dew. The exclamation point can be a diminutive act of defiance. It is how the silenced and overlooked shout in an email or in the blue bubble of a text on a cell phone. And a teenager's selfie might be one of the few ways they are able to define their fluid self.

15

Published in 1964, Susan Sontag's "Notes on Camp" is an essay in 58 sections. Across its many numbered parts, the text strives to define what camp is and isn't.

First of all, it's a sensibility, Sontag explains, one that loves "artifice and exaggeration."[16] It is also coded speech, a shibboleth for queer folk. Camp has style but rejects the demure (except, of course, when it makes a performance of being *very demure, very mindful*). No well-mannered pumps or severe black handbag for camp. Instead, camp is "a woman walking around in a dress made of three million feathers."[17] Camp is blue-eyeshadowed and stalks in stilettos.

Camp is enthusiastic too. It takes lavish pleasure in the pleasurable. It speaks with a voice that carries. It gesticulates grandly as if every room were an opera house and the second act was about to start, the red curtain parting, a lush hush of velvet.

16

As with Ngai's categories of the cute, the zany, and the interesting, Sontag's camp contains frivolity too. It "converts the serious into the frivolous," writes Sontag;[18] camp wants nothing more than to laugh at all the worst moments of being alive.

Although the essay is past sixty, much of Sontag's thesis remains relevant. The text reminds me that there are so many ways to say: *What you adore is a waste of time.* But camp doesn't care if others deem it inconsequential. Camp is indifferent to disdain. It pins a boutonniere to its damask suit and laughs. "Go fuck yourself, darling," it says, blowing a kiss from the door before it sashays away.

17

Sei Shōnagon's *The Pillow Book* is more than a thousand years old. The gentlewoman composed her daily observations in Japan's Heian period, an era rich in the visual arts and literary production. As a lady of Empress Teishi's court, Shōnagon had an intimate view of power, fine clothing, all the customs and ceremonies that busied courtiers' days. She wrote of what she saw in corridors, what she overheard from behind a painted screen, what she smelled in the folds of a brocade robe, whiffs of incense and star anise.

The translator Meredith McKinney observes that Shōnagon "has been dismissed by some as a mere chatterbox of a woman, and *The Pillow Book* considered to be nothing more than a silly gentlewoman's idle thoughts spilling themselves haphazardly on the page."[19] Those readers who defend Shōnagon's work, MicKinney writes, "are often characterized as vacuous and frivolous."

18

Central to *The Pillow Book* is the act of list-making. Shōnagon divides court life into idiosyncratic categories, including *Things that fall*, *Things that should be small*, and *Things of splendour and spectacle*. Quirky, minutely specific, her lists allow readers to enter a distant world that, as McKinney explains, remains "unimaginably different from ours" and "so opaque to us that often we have only her words to guide us."[20]

Of *Alarming-looking things*, Shōnagon records the following: "Thorny acorn husks. A hairy yam that's been baked. The prickly water lily. Water chestnuts. The sight of a man with a lot of hair, drying it after washing."[21] From this assemblage a reader might deduce that Shōnagon was distressed by the bristling and the furred, whatever is unruly.

19

The Pillow Book speaks most ardently about silken pleasures. Shōnagon is a connaisseuse of refinements. She is an expert in the sound of insects thrumming in the dark, a well-crafted poem sent by a lover, the smooth, white belly of a cat. In a section titled "Things of elegant beauty," she describes "a letter on fine green paper, tied to a sprig of willow covered in little bud leafs."[22] And later she references another letter, this one made of "violet paper, with a long cluster of wisteria blossom attached."[23]

In its adoration of trivialities, the book is a lesson in effective writing. It can be read as a manual for developing a poet's sensibility. With every concrete image, Shōnagon positions the reader inside the scene. Encountering her prose, I feel myself sitting so close to the letters tied with flowers that I can almost reach out to touch the colorful papers left on a table a thousand years ago—[24]

20

I don't keep a pillow book. But I do have a habit of making lists to sort the disarranged world into *do* and *done*. I write a list to prove that the hours are not a whisp of smoke. I write a list so that I can place a checkmark next to whatever resides in the past.

- Empty the dishwasher ✓
- Take out the trash ✓
- Walk the dogs ✓

By penning a mark on a page—its shape like a small incision carved in stone—I tell myself: *These minor tasks have significance.* No one else will notice I've bought milk and a carton of eggs, but my completed list offers proof. I exist in the imperatives and the check marks placed beside them.

21

Seven Ways to Drive Your Lover Wild. Ten Tips for Landing Your Dream Job. The Fifteen Most Iconic Shades of Red Lipstick.

22

Each of these could be the title for a listicle: a numbered essay constructed in the manner of a list. The listicle—a portmanteau of the words "list" and "article"—is a journalistic form often found on popular websites and in glossy magazines. It must have a catchy title to tempt a reader the way a bait box laid in a garden might appeal to a mouse, its lurid scent drifting through the weeds. A listicle isn't so much read as it is consumed, devoured by those who crave bite-sized pellets of language.

Writing about the listicle as a literary form, linguist Arika Okrent asserts:

> The necessary linearity of language imposes a struggle. To express ourselves we must make choices about what comes next, and that can be difficult. Listing makes this process easier. We can gather the items we need into one place and set them in a line, without worrying too much about the significance of the ordering or the transition from one item to the next. It accomplishes the first task, of breaking the world down into pieces, and gives it maybe not *the* path but *a* path to follow through them. Lists may not lead us to a deeper understanding of the world, but they give us the reassuring sense that understanding is at least possible.[25]

The listicle might be called the essence of frivolous writing. It is text as junk food, thoughts quickly swallowed.

But, as Okrent observes, the listicle offers comfort too. As a form, it makes an appealing argument: Complexity can be numbered. The most undigestible facts may be inventoried, however briefly. Our unruliest ideas and feelings may be cataloged, arranged one after the other in a register that reassures, *All things can be contained.*

23

Of course, certain lists are easy to recognize as serious. Lists of names chiseled on a monument, what we call *the fallen* from a distant war. Lists of families to be deported to a death camp located somewhere in the east. Lists of the missing after a storm.

These lists—concerned with death and the record-keeping of governments—are solemn, terrifying documents.

The more elusive list, however, is the one that appears slight on first encounter, an accounting barely worth the paper it's scribbled on.

24

Twenty-One Signs of Loneliness. Five More Stages of Grieving. Fifty Surprising Truths About Joy. One Hundred and One Reasons Frivolities Are Not Frivolous.

25

The list poem offers an inventory in verse. It names objects, action, events, or memories. Often the text includes exposition so that the poem pendulums between list-making and telling a story. Catalog / narrative / catalog / narrative. As the poem swings back and forth, the reader is forced to make sense out of fragment, the uneasy relationship between one item and the next.

Before the list poem came the litany, a singing language of magic and incantation. Litany, from the Greek *litaneia:* prayer. The litany supplicates. It entreats by repeating.

Take Jericho Brown's contemporary sonnet "The Tradition." It's a litany in which the speaker shifts between naming flowers and describing the experience of being a Black man in twenty-first century America. "*Aster. Nasturtium. Delphinium,*" the speaker begins.[26] And, later, he cites more flowers, the Latin words an enchantment, sugared in the mouth.

In between naming these fragrant blossoms, the speaker describes hands at work in a garden, planting perennials, how these efforts at cultivation are filmed, how the videos serve as an act of testimony and witness. The narrative moments in the poem feel dreamy, elusive as mist across the grasses. The poem closes with one more list. This time, the speaker doesn't name flowers cut down too soon but, rather, identifies three Black men, each one killed by police: "*John Crawford. Eric Garner. Mike Brown.*"

The clipped music of this final line sends me back to the beginning of the poem. Now, in rereading the text, the strange filming of the garden evokes the public's compulsive watching and rewatching of videos, those films in which police murder Black men. The recitation of exquisite flowers—each one beautiful, a slender stem slanting in a vase—becomes necessary to the sonnet's rhetoric. The poet summons the asters, nasturtiums, and delphiniums, so that later he can draw a parallel between the severed blossoms and the deaths of Crawford, Garner, and Brown.

In the same year that I tried to perfect my skin, more names could have been added to the poem's litany. *George Floyd. Daniel Prude. Andre Hill.*

The closing line of "The Tradition" reproaches. Much of the language is so beguiling—those flowers pinked and purpled, perfumed with myth—that the poem can lull with its frivolous blooms. The final line reminds the reader that not every incantation is meant to put us under its spell. Some litanies should shake us from insensible sleep. They should call us to action.

26

What if I were to write a defense of frivolity? What if I composed it as a list of perplexities? Because our lives are unbearably torn, I would say. Because we need diversion. Because pleasure. Because paradox.

27

I might argue that many things are less trivial than we might imagine. Or I would go further, saying that the utterly shallow parts of our lives offer beneficial, necessary distractions. I would claim that the entirely frivolous is essential too. Pure frivolity is like a palate cleanser—a small bowl of raspberry sorbet—that we consume before returning to the next somber course of a meal.

28

This list would make 101 points. Its form calls the reader's attention to the risks of dismissing an object, person, or pursuit as mere trifling.

On the one hand, we have a children's book like *The Hundred and One Dalmatians,* its pages filled with spotted fur and wagging tails. We have introductory college courses—English 101, Economics 101—with their thin overviews of complex matters.

But there is also the infamous room of torture, Room 101, in George Orwell's dystopian novel *1984*. Nothing lighthearted happens in that place: "The thing that is in Room 101 is the worst thing in the world. . . . It may be burial alive, or death by fire, or by drowning, or by impalement, or fifty other deaths. There are cases where it is some quite trivial thing, not even fatal."[27]

29

Perhaps, there would be gaps in my inventory, spots where the argument does not interlace perfectly with the one that came before. This is the nature of lists; they are nonlinear and fragmented. Then readers would have to stitch up each absence with new defenses of their own.

30

The list would wear lace and frills. Only by adorning itself in rich fabrics could the list persuade. Even the most austere reader can't help sliding a finger across a yard of green cloth, the nap of the fabric soft as moss and its thread the color of emeralds.

Here. Let me demonstrate the method:

31

According to the *OED,* the exclamation point was once known as the mark of admiration. It was a diacritic gesture that signified approval. It was an appreciative smile. It nodded and clapped, unreserved in its enthusiasm.

Now, in daily communications, the point indicates volume. It is a raised voice. A piercing *Oh!*

32

And it is to be avoided, at least if the author wants to be taken seriously. "I suggest that you use exclamation points rarely or not at all in formal writing," advises literary scholar Stephen Spector in *The Quotable Guide to Punctuation.* In *The Elements of Style,* William Strunk Jr. and E. B. White give this terse commandment: "Do not attempt to emphasize simple statements by using a mark of exclamation."[28]

To this decree, I say: *Well!!*

In ivory tower prose, the exclamation point resembles a flick of glitter. It shines like a Swarovski crystal glued to the end of a sentence, the writer's words bedazzled.

It is one of the least solemn of all punctuation marks. It is the sudden laughter in a dour conference room. It is the burst of applause in a concert hall. Everyone knows that the nocturne hasn't finished. But the exclamation point can't help itself and calls out, enraptured, *Oh, but the music is just so beautiful!*[29]

33

Further on, Spector writes, "Several studies since 1981 have shown that women use exclamation points far more often than men do, both online and in traditional writing."[30] He explains that one scholar concluded that "exclamation points are almost obligatory" for women who communicate in online discussions. "That's not because [the exclamation points] represent an outpowering of friendly feeling . . . but because not using them would seem unfriendly."

Journalist Emma Goldberg writes in the *New York Times* that "the exclamation point skews feminine."[31] Quoting linguist Gretchen McCulloch, she calls it a "social smile," explaining that it serves as a "mark of sincerity in a time when irony abounds."

34

I have felt this pressure to skew feminine in my own communications. I study a recent email sent to a colleague in my department—something about spreadsheets. There's the glitzy flash of an exclamation point in each paragraph. In this electronic correspondence, my use of exclamation points resembles the pleasant expression I fix to my face when walking a city street. Every day a stranger tells me to smile. Waiting for a light to switch from red to green at an intersection, I've heard a voice nearby. "Smile," the stranger calls out. The command comes from just beyond my peripheral vision. I don't need to see the speaker to know the shadowed threat of this moment. "Smile."

At such times, it's safest to rewrite my mouth into a syntax resembling happiness. It's not that I am experiencing "friendly feeling." It's simply that I'm afraid of what might happen if a man thought me hostile and decided to fold my face into a more pleasant look.

I feel this same fear in my professional life. I know what happens when a colleague sees me as unsmiling; I become the unaccompanied woman on the street, a creature who deserves to be targeted because she lacks warmth. In the classroom, my students expect maternal solicitude. I should offer them a plate of cookies or, better yet, a tray of homemade lasagna. When I have appeared too severe in my teaching, my pedagogy grim-faced, then my students complain at the end of the course. *Bitch,* they have written in my evaluations. *Cunt,* they have said.

"Smile," the stranger tells me as I wait to cross the street. "Smile," he repeats. And I do.

35

The writer Gertrude Stein can be counted among those prose stylists who have no patience for the frivolity of the exclamation point. In a lecture titled "Poetry and Grammar," she discusses which forms of punctuation "are interesting" and which "are not."[32]

First among the least is the question mark, Stein explains. "A question is a question," she writes, "anybody can know a question is a question and so why add to it the question mark when it is already there when the question is already there in the writing."[33] Exclamation points are equally unnecessary, not to mention that "they are ugly" and "they spoil the line of the writing."

Stein speaks about punctuation the way an architect might speak about a modern building. She is austere in her decrees. Nothing should mar the strict lines of the sentence's structure. No extraneous ornamentation. Only a grammar of glass and steel.

36

Not every poet feels as Stein does. Emily Dickinson, for instance, is famous for her exclamatory proclivities. True: The word "exclaim" appears only once in all the poems Dickinson is known to have written. It's in a poem that begins: "A *wounded* deer—leaps highest—."[34] The speaker offers a series of metaphors to explain how different beings and things work to conceal their pain. The deer that is hunted and wounded "leaps highest" in what turns out to be the moments before its dying. A piece of compressed metal coils in response to great pressure. A face pinkens—almost blushing—from a dangerous fever. And if we feel what Dickinson describes as "Anguish," we armor ourselves in "Mirth." Merriment is a shield we use, so that no one will notice our suffering and call out with sudden concern. Frivolity is a disguise.

I'm reading the version of "A *wounded* deer—leaps highest—" that appears in *The Poems of Emily Dickinson.* The book was edited by the distinguished scholar R. W. Franklin in 1998 and, more than two decades later, remains an essential contribution to the field. In his introduction, Franklin speaks passionately about his editorial approach:

> If the orthography, capitalization, punctuation, and usage should seem problematical, they are nonetheless Dickinson's, not the editor's or the publisher's, not, except indirectly, society's—agents with whom she conducted no negotiation toward public norms for her poetry. In this reading edition—a printed codex, a form familiar to her—the basic editorial choice has been either to follow her private intentions and characteristics, presenting the poems as well as transcription and the custom of typography can, or to lay onto the poems social conventions and judgements that were not hers. . . . The present one follows her own practice, selecting versions that focus on her latest full effort, adopting revisions and alternative readings for which she indicated a choice, and deferring to her custom in presentation and usage. The entry into her poetry is through her idiom.[35]

Her idiom, says Franklin. I feel the intimacy of his assertion, that the scholar believes he has come to know Dickinson through years of closeness with her words. No doubt he has touched the original drafts of her poems, leaned over the stitched pages in a quiet, temperature-controlled room. The archive has the hush of devotion. It is a place that can feel confidential, private as a bedroom.

As Franklin renders "A *wounded* deer—leaps highest –," there are five exclamation points in a text of only twelve lines. One appears at the end of the first stanza. There are three in the second quatrain. The last four lines close loudly, the exclamation point almost onomatopoetic. Franklin calls the poet's handling of punctuation "sylvan," as if the marks Dickinson makes are like the shadows cast by trees in an overgrown forest, the dashes and other characters branchlike.

37

Like so many American poets, I've dreamed about Dickinson's quiet life. I can easily summon from memory that daguerreotype of a young Emily cinched in a black gown, a striped ribbon at her neck, one arm leaning on a tablecloth, her hands clasping a nosegay. There's a book at her elbow. Her fingers are delicate. Her mouth—what is that expression she makes? Amusement, I think, barely contained.[36]

Her papers were furious or terrified or full of questions. Her words, although unpublished, were often so loud. Many have ridiculed Dickinson for the strangeness of her choices. All those dashes. All those fanciful exclamation points. She belonged to an era in which all women writers were perceived as frivolous, a "damned mob of scribbling women,"[37] as Nathaniel Hawthorne wrote in 1855. Her punctuation sometimes signals the conclusion of a sentence, the pauses in syntax, the hesitations. And this is what aggravates some readers: the idiosyncrasies of her exclamations. The marks often indicate an eyebrow arched in skepticism. But they are also a hand placed over a mouth to muffle laughter. They are a narrowing, critical gaze.

38

Now let me direct my gaze to another feminine figure.

The girl is nearly submerged. Waves crest to her chin. One arches over her head; its silvery, frilled edge mirrors the pair of tears that squeeze from her eyes. She lifts a hand barely out of the ocean, as if reaching for help, almost too tired to go on treading water. Her dark hair, an elegant bob, is tinted blue with shadow. Perhaps, she's illuminated by the moon, which gazes down at her from some dispassionate position in the sky. "I don't care!" reads the thought bubble floating to the left of her head. "I'd rather sink—than call Brad for help!"

Roy Lichtenstein painted *Drowning Girl* in 1963. He took the image of the sinking girl from a comic book published the year before, cropped out a ship in the background, the boyfriend as well, and left behind only the young woman. Her face is now huge and illustrated. The artist's paints appear flat as ink printed from a drum, the canvas pulp-like. Thousands of tiny dots fill the composition, the artist having stenciled each one on, a time-consuming mimicry of the Ben-Day dots used in mechanical printing.

Lichtenstein would become famous for his refigurations of comic books, single frames and sometimes panels enlarged so that these two-dimensional narratives about love or war could be read differently, treated with the same reverence that viewers so often give to paintings hung in a museum. The critic Arthur Danto explains that the artist "had a revolutionary agenda"[38] and wished "to bring vernacular art in the art gallery, which until then had been open only to fine art." He argues that Lichtenstein's paintings are "unique." The painter's hand makes intentional, specific marks on canvas. His work is meticulous. Those marks resemble the technologies used to produce disposable, inexpensive text. But they are not equally disposable, Danto says. "We wrap food in the funny papers, or dump coffee grounds in them—but it would be barbarism to do such things"[39] with one of Lichtenstein's paintings. A viewer encounters the mass-produced, now reinvented as fine art, and is asked to reconsider its frivolity.

39

When I look at other pieces from the same period, such as *Bratatat!*, *Whaam!*, and *Varoom!*, what I notice are the exclamation points. Lichtenstein uses the punctuation mark in the same way as do the writers of the comic books from whom he is borrowing. The exclamation points are onomatopoetic. They imitate the blast of an explosion, the staccato sound of guns firing from a fighter jet.

In *Drowning Girl*, the exclamation points have another function. They convey the young woman's petulance, that she would rather die than call out to Brad. And who is this Brad anyway? With an insipid name like that, he hardly seems up to the challenge of a rescue. Therefore, the girl keeps drowning, fixed forever to the canvas, her face romantic and doomed, her choice not to be saved one that strikes me as simultaneously foolish and poignant. Even in danger, the pinup girl remains perfectly coiffed, while underneath the waves, she flutters her slender legs, those pale and shapely feet.

She opts for helplessness rather than being helped by a man. In her sinking, she insists on bodily autonomy. She pointedly rejects what the comic books tell us she so desires: the heft of bulging biceps, a masculine flash of white teeth.

40

I wonder what Lichtenstein would make of the selfie, our modern form of portraiture, these quick pictures snapped in private and public places, the cellphone's camera turned back on the photographer. Selfies are the new mirrors. They require a long arm.

41

In the Year of Perfect Skin, I held the lens as far from my body as possible. Then, with a fumbling thumb, I pressed a button to claim the image—*you're mine!* There was my face in miniature before me, like a likeness painted on glass, no longer on vellum but a digital signal. Impermanent permanence.

42

In the time of our global pandemic, I began to watch myself. Those were the months of learning how to do work over video, all conversations held in digital boxes, each head contained by a rectangular frame, and always my own image fixed in the top right corner of the screen.

Studying myself on the computer—a living, moving selfie, the dysphoria of that view—forced me to meet an unfamiliar face. This wasn't the same reflection I found in a bathroom mirror. Instead, I saw someone reversed: my face as others encountered it every day, but distorted by the camera, my nose widened, my chin a blunt obstruction.

My vanity was an interference. It distracted me.[40] I thought of those still life paintings from the Renaissance, images of tables set with slowly rotting fruit, a silver fish on a plate, the pelt of an animal. On the computer screen, I was stilled as well. *All is vanity*, those antique pictures warn. They caution the viewer: *You are mortal, you are aging, you will die.*

For twenty dollars, I bought a ring of light. The glowing circle flattened my features into a bright, uncanny smoothness. I bought a metal stand to prop my laptop at the perfect height. In the video settings, I discovered a filter that could "touch up my appearance." All I had to do was push the slider as far as it could go, and my whole face blurred into soft focus like a movie star in a film from the 1940s. Now beautified, I could forget myself again. I could communicate without watching constantly my own self-portrait, that pixelated woman in unappealing miniature.

43

Think of the queen in the story "Little Snow White." A reader could argue that her obsession with beauty is shallow. After all, doesn't she have a whole kingdom to rule, affairs of state to conduct? The queen sits on a high thrown. She commands an army that has thousands of spears. She holds a scepter and wears a crown sharp with rubies.

Why worry about her ranking among the fair? Why should the superlative—*fairest*—matter to a woman with so much sway?

Why? The queen understands that gender is linked like a thin gold chain to power, and a woman's power is easily snapped apart. When the queen fusses about beauty, she is worrying about her influence in the world. The mirror tells her, *This is the extent of your sovereignty*. Each day, a new crease in the brow. Each day, her dominion decreases.

44

In Jack Zipes's translation of the fairy tale, the queen keeps failing to murder her own daughter, a girl she had once wished for: "If only I had a child as white as snow, as red as blood, and as black as the wood of the window frame!"[41] The existence of such loveliness pulls at the delicate chain of the queen's power. And in response to this threat, she repeatedly attempts to kill Little Snow White.

But the huntsman can't bring himself to stab the girl in the forest. And, later, the dwarfs undo a strangling ribbon from around the child's neck. They remove a poisoned comb from Little Snow White's hair. The deadly apple is knocked from her throat by a servant in the palace of a prince. The story seems to argue that beauty can bring good luck. The girl's perfect face saves her so many times.

At the end of the fairy tale—Little Snow White now married—the queen's feet are bound in "iron slippers" that have been "heated over a fire."[42] As punishment, she is forced to dance at the wedding feast, her toes and heals blistering with the pain of these metal shoes, until she dances herself "to death."

A second lesson of the story: You will be admonished for your loss of beauty. You will be made to hurt, made uglier, until that hideousness means unbearable pain and a blistered ending.[43]

45

Girl. Then woman. Then crone.

Right now, I sit somewhere between the second and third of these roles. I am not quite an evil queen, although the mirror often fills me with fury. I am a woman in her early fifties, already feeling the diminution of a particular kind of power, a decrease of influence which comes with the deepening of creases around my mouth. They are known as marionette lines, as if my face were carved out of wood and I were a puppet. Time manipulates the strings, and my limbs move obediently.

On social media, I watch a woman in her sixties drag concealer across the furrows of her forehead, beneath her eyes, and around her mouth. She daubs a sponge in the shape of a teardrop over the makeup until the tint seems to disappear into her skin. *See,* she asks her incorporeal audience, *see how much younger I look?*

These are the new mirrors—our phones and what they reflect of our anxieties and desires. Algorithms are guided by heuristic functions. They give us more and more of what we want, even if what we desire is to wince with self-loathing. Heuristic comes from the Greek εὑρίσκειν, to discover. Through the algorithms of social media, we unearth new disgusts. Our faces and bodies are like stones overturned in a garden; beneath, we find centipedes and skittering beetles. We encounter these dank, muddy parts of ourselves and want to roll back the rocks, to keep uncovering the repulsive.

46

When I reflect on it, my own girlhood often comes back to me as a series of pink visions. I loved a doll who wore a puffy pink bonnet tied around the poof of her pink plastic hair. My favorite dessert was a cake polka-dotted with the pink of maraschino cherries sliced into rounds. When we ate at fancy restaurants, I always ordered a Shirley Temple, the swirl of grenadine syrup sliding into the soda's fizz, the pink twisting in the carbonation, until I stirred it with a swizzle stick and the drink turned to a flushed shade of dawn.

"Only in the relatively recent past did pink acquire its feminine connotations," writer Anna Broadway clarifies in an essay about the color's history in fashion.[44] It wasn't until the late 1980s, for instance, that children's clothing became coded by color, accorded to gender. Pink for girls. Blue for boys. A rigid binary.

As Broadway writes, the early 1990s gave us the "now ubiquitous" pink ribbon of Breast Cancer Awareness

Month. I came of age in those years. Pink was now not only the color of girls and women but also the hue of what might kill us.

47

The artist David Batchelor argues that "in the West, since Antiquity, colour has been systematically marginalized, reviled, diminished and degraded."[45] He gives a name to this "fear of corruption" via the colorful: *chromophobia*. Color, he writes, is seen as belonging to a "foreign body," which usually means "the feminine, the oriental, the primitive, the infantile, the vulgar, the queer or the pathological." Color poses a threat or else "it is trivial, or it is both."[46]

Cultural historian Kassia St. Clair makes a similar claim about color's low standing in Western culture: "Color was a distraction from the true glories of art: line and form. It was seen as self-indulgent and, later, sinful: a sign of dissimulation and dishonesty."[47] As for pink, St. Clair explains that "it is seen as simultaneously infantilizing and, ever since artists first put mixtures of cochineal, ocher, and white to canvas to depict naked female flesh, sexualizing."[48]

So, pink is dangerous. It's the pigment of frivolity. It's childish and carnal, juvenile and disingenuous.

48

Given what David Batchelor says, it should come as no surprise that pink also signifies queerness, the cost of being queer, the risks. Public historian Jake Newsome writes about the complex evolution of the pink triangle:

> Originating as a concentration camp badge, the pink triangle was used by the Nazi SS (Schutzstaffel) to identify men imprisoned in concentration camps for being gay. For those men, the pink triangle meant torture, degradation, humiliation, and in all too many cases, death. Decades later, gay activists—first in West Germany and then in the United States—imbued the symbol with new meaning as they fought for legal and social equality. . . . In the context of gay activism, queer communities transformed the pink triangle from a badge of damnation, shame, and imprisonment into a visual marker of resistance, pride, and liberation.[49]

Gay men were made to wear that infamous badge in the Nazi death camps. The triangles stitched to their uniforms stood precariously on point, fragile forms:

▼

Later, in the 1980s, during the early years of the AIDS epidemic, queer protesters held signs marked with pink triangles. SILENCE = DEATH, the placards read. But now the shape was reoriented, no longer uneasy or fragile but placed on its steady, defiant base:

▲

49

Pink can be found everywhere in nature: flowers, a certain moment in the morning sky, a handful of precious gemstones. The color is associated with some parts of some human bodies and some animals as well, pigs for instance, baby mice, flamingoes perched in a pool of turquoise water. Depending on skin tone, pink can appear on a face as embarrassment or desire, also excitement, perhaps terror at times. But despite its omnipresence in many parts of the natural world, for human beings pink has frequently taken on a very narrow meaning, one of femininity and feminization.

50

There's Barbie, for example. She was the first mass-produced doll to be sold in the shape of a woman instead of an infant. Before Barbie, dolls were life-sized babies. They taught little girls how to be mommies, how to change a diaper, how to burp a fussy newborn. Before Barbie, dolls functioned:

- as effigies
- as talismans
- as figures of the uncanny

Barbie doesn't check these boxes. Less than a foot tall and yet somehow entirely mature, she provides diminutive lessons in adulthood. She doesn't offer instructions in the maternal. Hers is a curriculum of fashion, career, and love affairs.

If Barbie does resemble a baby doll, it's that she too might serve as a companion. But she doesn't need nurturing. Barbie herself is motherless. She will not be rocked in a little girl's arms, no lullaby singing her to sleep.

As a child, how many times did I hold a Barbie and Ken, one doll in each hand, and knock them together at their waists, making kissy-kissy noises as a way of understanding the grownup stuff that I could barely name, matters of love and desire? Or I took two Barbies and placed them together in bed, angled limb to the angled limb; I tried to imagine myself in such intimacy, what it might feel like for a plastic hand to touch a plastic breast. I walked Barbie in little bouncing steps across the floor of my bedroom. Would my hips move one day with such va-va-voom, the seductive movements of this doll?

Barbie has an elongated form designed to look good in stylish clothes. Some women dream of having an hourglass figure. And then there are Barbie's proportions, her unattainable ratios of bust to waist to hips. Those legs are infinite and end with a pair of tiny feet eternally perched on tiptoe to accommodate the knifepoint height of heels. Or, as writer Maria Teresa Hart observes in her book *Doll*, "Barbie's body is bonkers."[50] Her shape bonks us with its disproportion. She seems boinkable, prepared for boinking anywhere, up for anything, as someone crass might say. Hart explains: "When I take Barbie's body into my own hands, I don't see a molded figure so much as a prism. We beam into this object an ideal of womanhood, and what gets refracted out is a spectrum of beauty standards, sexual fantasies, consumer excess, and racial categorization."[51]

Barbie's logo has always been pink, a signature swirl of fuchsia. The color can be found in the Pantone Matching

System—PMS as it's known—as number 219C. Categorized as a shade of magenta pink, 219C is vivid. It's not unobtrusive. It isn't modest or restrained. It has the intensity of extreme embarrassment or passionate arousal.

It's also a shade that provokes strong responses. In an essay about the color, fashion critic Vanessa Friedman condemns it as the nadir of all pinks:

> First came millennial pink, that comforting dusty rose pink that reflected a generational and dual gender nostalgia for the swaddling innocence of childhood. Then the bright pink of the pussy hat pink, a rebellious, in-your-face-pink of feminine protest. And now, Barbie pink, the most artificial, commercialized, almost tacky, unmistakable pink of all.[52]

Friedman writes this critique shortly after the blockbuster release of the *Barbie* movie. By this point, pink was everywhere. It saturated the summer of 2023, tinging our days with a bubblegum glow. "I am choking on pink," complains Friedman. "Drenched in pink."

51

Two films came out on the same day, *Oppenheimer* from Universal Pictures and *Barbie* from Warner Bros. The public was amused by the juxtaposition of these two flicks, the one so evidently serious and the other so clearly frivolous. Attending both was an experience that birthed a portmanteau: Barbenheimer. This double billing seemed to offer audiences a binary. *Oppenheimer* was a portrait of masculine genius, its central themes war and power. *Barbie* was an azalea-hued retelling of Pinocchio, the doll's adventures in the human world allowing her to become a real woman-child. What could be more profound a story than the development of the first atomic bombs? And what could be sillier than the tale of a beloved plastic doll brought to life, every iconic part of her given form on the big screen?

In their opening weekend, the two films made hundreds of millions of dollars, with *Barbie* far outperforming *Oppenheimer*. During the 2024 awards season, it was *Oppenheimer* that won in numerous categories. And *Barbie*? It failed to receive such critical recognition.

But for all its pink-tinged marketing, *Barbie* isn't exactly as frivolous as audiences had anticipated initially. What to do, for instance, with its references to Proust and patriarchy, its delicate examination of Ken's masculinity? The character sings and dances and turns briefly tyrannical, all his actions an effort to persuade Barbie: *Love me, please, love me.*

Or maybe the movie is serious (about frivolity). That summer, people laughed and clapped in the theaters. They came to showings dressed in their finest renditions of Barbie fashion, wearing pink leggings, pink crop tops, pink heels and sneakers. Meanwhile, scholars and critics couldn't reach a consensus. Some saw the film as sly and subversive. Some thought it exploitative.

In her review, Helen O'Hara writes of Barbie Land, where much of the movie takes place: "It's not a feminist utopia, because that would be more equal, but a hilarious upending of our own reality. This is a world where pink is a totally normal, serious colour, instead of being treated as somehow frivolous because it's associated with little girls."[53] The writer Chavisa Woods condemns the work. The "*Barbie* movie is so insidious because much of it was incredibly enjoyable," she argues. "It is a true masterpiece of capitalism. It is visually gorgeous. The most highly qualified people in the film industry worked on this movie. It enjoyed a nearly unlimited budget."[54] Carol Hay, a professor of philosophy, characterizes *Barbie* as "queer camp" and explains:

> Today's mainstream visibility of trans women has played an important role in advancing the cultural conversation about the respectability of femininity. Some anti-trans critics accuse the unapologetic femininity of trans women of entrenching retrograde stereotypes. Their femmephobia seems to prevent them from realizing that the objects of their scorn could be celebrating femininity, not denigrating it.[55]

And queer film critic Juan Barquin praises *Barbie* for its ability to entertain, even as the film offers a nuanced and complex examination of what it means to be a person. None of us is easily packaged, he says:

> The fact that we can be both frivolous and complicated, or pink and black, or high heel and Birkenstock, or whatever other nonsensical dichotomy, like "commercial" and "art," one might pick—are impossible to box up. . . . *Barbie* may not provide any answers, nor will it spark the same feeling of recognition in everyone who watches it, but it may very well help someone forget how suffocating the world's problems and its unreasonable expectations are, if only for a couple of hours.[56]

Even years later, I still can't decide what to think about *Barbie*. What I do know, however, is that the movie's frivolity is a costume. It may have a color palette that evokes bubblegum and flamingos but, as the critics demonstrate, it's a work that can withstand close reading.

52

Timothy Schaffert, the author of such novels as *The Titanic Survivors Book Club* and *The Perfume Thief*, is a writer who would certainly be characterized as serious. Yet, in his free time, he creates what he calls "candy-wrapper drawings."[57] Using pencil, some kind of adhesive, and the old packaging from chocolates and candies, Schaffert makes illustrations that merge fashion, celebrity, and confection. He posts these images to social media, the illustrations full of humor and intelligence, like modern-day portrait miniatures.

Here is Myrna Loy looking slinky in a gown made of purple and gold candy wrappers from Godiva truffles. Here's Marlene Dietrich in a pink crinkle of foil, a cigarette lofting curlicues of smoke. And here's Tallulah Bankhead in the green folds of a hazelnut chocolate wrapper.

Speaking over video conference, Schaffert explained to me that although he had made these drawings for many years, it was only during the pandemic that they became a daily practice. Shortly before social distancing and our great communal confinement began, he bought a great bagful of Italian chocolates that lent themselves to fashion: "And then came lockdown. I was also diagnosed with mini-strokes around the same time. I had some memory loss, and focusing on these illustrations really allowed me to step away from the frustrations that I was having."

Schaffert draws with a dollar-store mechanical pencil, the plastic kind that come in cheap packages by the hundreds. He finds high fashion where most people would see little pieces of trash. And while writing novels requires "intensive intellectual engagement," the candy-wrapper drawings make different demands on his creativity: "They allow me to go into a space where I'm just thinking about the pleasure of feeling a pencil against a piece of paper. I'm just thinking in terms of color—I try to see which wrappers lend themselves to the luminosity of fabric and the drama of a gown."

During our conversation, I asked Schaffert what he has discovered in drawing hundreds of movie stars and famous singers and public figures. What has he learned from clothing these iconic bodies in little scraps of metallic paper, disposable materials that were never intended to be transmuted into haute couture? His answer surprised me:

> I've learned how much the same our faces are, how everybody to a certain degree looks alike, in the sense that most of us have two eyes and a nose and a mouth. The shapes of our faces are much the same. The process of contemplating what makes each of us distinctive is something that I can't articulate in words. But I feel like it's something that I can capture through these illustrations.

I am struck by the tenderness of Schaffert's project—this attention paid to what makes a face a face. During the pandemic, I pursued the diversion of perfecting my skin; Schaffert grappled instead with the technical challenges of rendering these portraits. Candy wrappers, as he explained to me, are "designed not to stick." But it's their very "lack of cooperation" that can lead to something beautiful in its ephemerality, crinkling plastic manipulated to resemble the radiant folds of satin or silk.

53

Maybe, one day, Schaffert will consider drawing a few of my favorite literary heroines. I would like to see Elizabeth Bennet draped in cream-colored candy-bar wrappers, the waxy paper like a simple muslin dress. Becky Sharp could wear a gown crafted of red tinfoil. Certainly, Emma Bovary—famous for her shopping sprees—would look lovely if costumed in the lush packaging of a high-end chocolate truffle.

Novelist Michèle Roberts characterizes Bovary as "utterly modern."[58] Of Flaubert's creation, Roberts says:

> It's the first sex-and-shopping novel, after all. Emma Bovary, desperately seeking satisfaction and fulfilment, employs retail therapy as an escape from an unhappy marriage, experiments with adultery, is obsessed with money and with material objects as substitutes for happiness. She's convinced it's men who've got it all: power and freedom and choice and ease of movement. She can't buy herself the male privileges she envies, so she spends money on blue glass vases and new curtains instead.

In part 2, chapter 7, for example, Emma is heartbroken at Léon Dupuis's departure for Paris. At this point in the novel, Emma is already married to Charles but has hazy erotic feelings for Léon. As they discover when they first meet earlier in the book, the two young people share romantic ideals about art, literature, and the kind of natural landscape that "raises up the soul and feeds a feeling of infinity."[59] After many pages of unconsummated desire and increasing sexual frustration, Léon goes to Paris, where he plans to study law. Emma responds to this loss by shopping:

> She bought a Gothic prie-dieu, and in one month she spent fourteen francs on lemons for cleaning her nails; she wrote off to Rouen, to order a blue cashmere dress; she chose the very best scarf from Lheureux; she tied it round her waist over her dressing-gown; then, with the shutters closed, and a book in her hand, she would recline on a sofa in her accoutrements.[60]

For Emma, shopping is a release. It's an activity that approximates freedom and agency. Corseted by the constraints of marriage and motherhood, she tries to express herself through her gowns, the knickknacks she purchases for her home, the perfume she dabs on her neck.

Part of the pleasure of reading Flaubert lies in the granular specificity of his prose. Even when Emma is depicted as irresponsible, selfish, self-absorbed, she remains fascinating and fully believable as a character. Her spending habits, her increasingly elaborate outfits, and her tastes in books all tend toward the frivolous. She is also real.[61] She is a portrait rendered in Flaubert's precise and critical brushstrokes, every flaw alive in those pages.

54

Jane Austen holds a more complex view of shopping and fashion than does Flaubert. She is sympathetic to the fact that her heroines care about the feel of fabrics or whether a dress is well-cut. Austen understands why the women in her world worry about skirts and bonnets and carved brooches. Appearance matters. Beauty determines a woman's marital prospects. A fine face or a pleasing figure can mean an advantageous match. High cheekbones and a lovely mouth can rescue a whole family from destitution. Or, as Mrs. Bennet tells her daughter Jane in *Pride and Prejudice:* "I knew how it would be. I always said it must be so, at last. I was sure you could not be so beautiful for nothing!"[62] And that's the point: In Austen's world, beauty is useful. The right hairdo. A grosgrain ribbon strategically placed. These things might mean the difference between spinsterhood and a comfortable life on a country estate, the garden hedges pruned to the right degree of wildness.

In *Northanger Abbey,* for example, Catherine Morland is so taken with the swift narrative turns of gothic novels that she often misreads social interactions. Her taste in silly, superficial literature leads her to behave in ways that are equally juvenile. Early in the book, we see her swept up in giddy contemplations of clothing:

> What gown and what head-dress she should wear on the occasion became her chief concern. She cannot be justified in it. Dress is at all times a frivolous distinction, and excessive solicitude about it often destroys its own aim. Catherine knew all this very well; her great aunt had read her a lecture on the subject only the Christmas before; and yet

> she lay awake ten minutes on Wednesday night debating between her spotted and her tamboured muslin, and nothing but the shortness of the time prevented her buying a new one for the evening.[63]

It's clear that Austen is poking fun at her young protagonist. Catherine's flaw is not that she cares about dresses but that she's carried away by silken thoughts of embroidery. Austen prefers her heroines to be restrained and modest. They must be pretty but not overly concerned with bonnets, gloves, and two-toned cameo pendants.

55

Catherine Morland is a lover of novels, sometimes overcome by the twists of gothic plotlines, the prose purple as cut amethysts. But ultimately, she is also a sweet girl. Other characters in Austen's novels are judged more harshly for their preoccupations with the frivolous. In *Emma,* the exasperating Mrs. Elton comes from vulgar new money. She is loud. She has brash opinions. And because Austen can't resist allowing her worst characters to behave badly, she lets Mrs. Elton speak in the novel's closing paragraph:

> The wedding was very much like other weddings, where the parties have no taste for finery or parade; and Mrs. Elton, from the particulars detailed by her husband, thought it all extremely shabby, and very inferior to her own.— "Very little white satin, very few lace veils; a most pitiful business!—Selina would stare when she heard of

> it."—But, in spite of these deficiencies, the wishes, the hopes, the confidence, the predictions of the small band of true friends who witnessed the ceremony, were fully answered in the perfect happiness of the union.[64]

Mrs. Elton is the voice of crassness and poor taste. Her criticism of the wedding party reveals not only her superficiality but also that she believes in excess, in glittering displays of wealth. Affluence should be flaunted. A rich bride must be draped in pearls, her dress heavy with beading. Anything less than ostentation is a sign of weak judgment.

In contrast, Emma Woodhouse—who is perhaps Austen's most imperfect and interesting protagonist—chooses understatement and refinement. For all her failings, Emma comes to care less about fashion and its uses as a mark of social status, a way of putting her inferiors in their place. She loses much of her snobbishness as she falls in love with Mr. Knightley and becomes his "own Emma, by hand and word."[65]

56

Of course, fashion is used to express character in *Pride and Prejudice* too. In one of the novel's funnier moments, Elizabeth Bennet marches across a pasture to Netherfield Park where her sister Jane is convalescing, having caught a cold in the rain. When Lizzie arrives at the estate, the Bingley sisters are horrified at the state of her petticoat "six inches deep in mud, . . . and the gown which had been let down to hide it, not doing its office."[66] The two women view Elizabeth's indifference to dress as a shocking violation.

Doesn't she know her primary duty is to avoid all exertions, any effort that might result in a torn hem?

Toward the end of the novel, Mrs. Bennet talks about buying a trousseau for her daughter Lydia, who has run off with the rake George Wickham. The couple narrowly avoids scandal by marrying in a rushed ceremony. But Mrs. Bennet can only think of "those attendants of elegant nuptials, fine muslins, new carriages, and servants."[67] She is oblivious to the disaster her family has just avoided, seemingly unaware of her daughter's improprieties. Mr. Bennet, on the other hand, is adamant that he will "not encourage the impudence of either" his daughter or his new son-in-law. There will be no lavish trousseau:

> Mrs. Bennet found, with amazement and horror, that her husband would not advance a guinea to buy clothes for his daughter. He protested that she should receive from him no mark of affection whatever on the occasion. Mrs. Bennet could hardly comprehend it. That his anger could be carried to such a point of inconceivable resentment as to refuse his daughter a privilege without which her marriage would scarcely seem valid, exceeded all she could believe possible. She was more alive to the disgrace which her want of new clothes must reflect on her daughter's nuptials, than to any sense of shame at her eloping and living with Wickham a fortnight before they took place.[68]

Austen uses a debate about clothing to show the Bennets' fundamental incompatibility. These two people have been married for decades, but they barely possess self-knowledge, much less knowledge of each other. While Mr. Bennet is horrified that his daughter's dishonor has been covered up "with so little inconvenience to himself," Mrs. Benet is unable to recognize how close the whole family came to social ruin.

57

Nearly ninety years after the publication of *Pride and Prejudice,* economist Thorstein Veblen examines the topic of clothing in *The Theory of the Leisure Class.* Veblen defines the leisure class as those so wealthy they do not need to work; they are exempt from what he calls "industrial occupations."[69] Freed from the exhaustion of labor, members of the leisure class devote themselves to collecting possessions and to engaging in refined, elegant idleness. Conspicuous consumption and conspicuous leisure, as Veblen names these two pursuits, allow the leisure class to exhibit prestige and riches, not to mention contempt for the drudgery of earning a paycheck.

In "Dress as an Expression of the Pecuniary Culture," Veblen explains that, for the leisure class, clothing serves to "make plain to all observers that the wearer is not engaged in any kind of productive labour."[70] A hat, a glove, a shoe must not only be beautiful, spotless, and costly. It must also project that "the wearer cannot when so attired bear a hand in any employment that is directly and immediately of human use." Each expensive item is what Veblen scathingly calls an "insignia of leisure," a badge that announces one is "consuming without producing."

As Veblen sees it, women's dress is far more extreme than men's attire in "demonstrating the wearer's abstinence from productive employment."[71] *The Theory of the*

Leisure Class was written during the Gilded Age, when women's bodies were forced into exaggerated, corseted forms, the bustles huge beneath their embroidered skirts, their mutton sleeves puffed at the shoulder and confining at the wrist. Necessary accoutrements would have included a fan, a glittering brooch, a hat perched on a coiled hill of hair. Veblen observes that a woman of the leisure class must—according to the dictates of fashion—wear a skirt that "hampers the wearer at every turn and incapacitates her for all useful exertion." Worst of all, this exquisite and constraining clothing is meant to show a woman's "economic dependence" on a man.[72] Each dress is a material representation of her husband's or her father's enormous wealth. Restrictive, confining, at times reducing her to "physical infirmity," her sublime garments mark her as "the chief menial of the household."

I suspect that Veblen would agree with Jane Austen's assessments of Mrs. Elton and the sisters Bingley. These are superficial women who place too much value on the importance of dress. They are so concerned with what a satin gown must signify in social circles that they miss all the ways in which high fashion is a symbol of their subjugation.

58

After the worst of the pandemic, when I finally left my house and returned to the classroom, to the office, to other public spaces, I no longer knew what to wear. Clothing has always been a way for me to announce myself. *I love color,* my scarf might say. *I am attracted to quiet forms of communication,* says the swish of my black silk skirt.

But now I didn't know what my outfits should express. After many months of wondering whether such uncertainties really mattered, I hired a personal stylist who helps people revise their closets, edit their outfits as if our clothing might become shapely, elegant pieces of prose. Dacy Gillespie teaches her clients how to shop mindfully and how to dress for themselves instead of for the narrowed, searing gaze of other people. In our meetings, we discussed how I wanted to feel about fashion. We talked about why I shop for pleasure, the allure of tissue paper folded around a new sweater, the tiny tap of a credit card touching a bright screen. We considered which parts of my body I try to conceal beneath huge swoops of fabric.[73]

More recently, I spoke with Gillespie during a video conference. I had heard her express anxieties about working as a stylist and wanted to understand how she found a way to pursue this love of clothing, despite her fear of being labeled frivolous.

Raised in Mobile, Alabama, Gillespie collected fashion magazines and followed every trend. But her parents were union organizers; as a little girl, she recognized that her passion for clothing would not lead to a job that "directly saved lives" and that her family expected her to "go into something political," a practical, substantive profession. [74]

By her mid-thirties, Gillespie was in therapy for depression and realized that she still wanted a life in fashion. And even today, as an accomplished business owner, she continues to struggle with telling other people about her work: "My father—who is 76—does not know what I do for a living. I'm just too afraid of judgment. I'm afraid that he would say, *Who on earth would pay someone to do that?* That's his voice in my head."

During our talk, I asked Gillespie how she would respond to accusations of frivolity. How would she counteract critiques about her work? "One, we all have to wear clothes," she explained. "And two, if you can get some pleasure out of that—why not? The world has always needed beauty and art in it. And there are people whose job it is to enable or provide the beautiful through the art of clothing. I enable."

And that's the thing about fashion. It "thrives on contradiction," historian Rebecca Arnold writes:

> By some, it is seen as rarefied and elite, a luxury world of couture craftsmanship and high-end retailers. For others, it is fast and throwaway, available on every high street. . . . It inhabits intellectual texts and renowned museums, but can be seen in television makeover shows and dedicated websites. It is this very ambiguity that makes it fascinating, and which can also provoke hostility and disdain.[75]

In this way, fashion seems the perfect embodiment of frivolity in general. All frivolous pursuits are burdened with paradox. Arnold insists that fashion "is a vibrant form of visual and material culture that plays an important role in our social and cultural lives."[76] "It shapes our bodies, and the way we look at other people's bodies," she explains. "It can enable creative freedom to express alternative identities, or dictate what is deemed beautiful and acceptable." Doesn't Emma Bovary—despite her deficiencies, how difficult she is for a reader to admire or like—prove the point? It's through the spending of money, particularly on charming, lovely dresses, that Emma can wage her minor rebellion. Every dainty pair of gloves, every embroidered handkerchief is a delicate declaration of the self.

Clothes, as the adage goes, make the man. In an essay titled "Why Are Pants So Big (Again)?" writer Jonah Weiner investigates his own humorous preoccupations with what he wears:

> To state what's obvious, I care a lot about pants. I'm tempted to say that I care too much about them, because we often frame a preoccupation with clothes as vain, frivolous and otherwise regrettable. It certainly can be those things. But I try to make sense of it as an abiding fascination with the beautiful, funny, fraught workings of a visual language that all of us speak all the time, deftly or ineptly, consciously or not.[77]

Despite what Veblen might have to say about my conspicuous consumption, I too care a lot about my pants. Also my scarves. Also my coats and blazers, the mother-of-pearl buttons that dot the edge of my leopard-print blouse. People who worry about fashion usually have what we call *an eye for detail*. That is, *they sweat the small stuff*. They think about *the little things*. Meticulousness is valued in architects and brain surgeons. But lovers and makers of clothing? No. When it comes to the cut of a wool suit or the drape of a bodice, that kind of exacting attention is considered frivolous.

Nonetheless, the clothing we put on our bodies tells others what we defy and what we believe. A woman might be beaten or executed for the cloth she refuses to drape across her face. Another might be assaulted in a bar, a white pill dropped into her drink, the rest of the night a drugged swirl of unconsent. When the assailant is questioned, the shortness of a woman's skirt becomes a defense. *Well, she asked for it*, the rapist might say.

59

"Some human artifacts seem to possess the powers of display and seduction that are proper to living things," philosophy professor Barbara Carnevali observes in her book Social Appearances. "Highly communicative accessories like ornaments, jewelry, and clothes can be viewed as animate objects, as actively contributing to their wearers' presentation and effectively influencing external situations."[78] All these frivolous adornments come alive on our bodies. They are animated by their contact with our warmth and movement. The gold hoops in our ears, the pair of blue satin pumps barely fixed to our feet—these things become as much a part of who we are as do our gesticulations, certain intonations of the voice.

Carnevali explains that "appearance is basically a fabric caught between two conflicting, equally powerful impulses: displaying versus concealing, public versus private, vanity versus shame and *decoration* versus *decorum*."[79] What we choose to wear is no longer a matter of mere ostentation or diversion. Clothing reveals our aspirations. We are told to *dress for the job you want*. Clothing also conceals the vulnerable parts of our bodies: the genitals, the jiggling lumps, the zones of our skin that are suddenly seen as erotic or obscene, depending on the fashion and the year.

60

I learned to love clothing from my Oma who was a skilled dressmaker. After the imposition of the Nuremberg Laws in 1933, she was forced to give up her plans to move to

Paris, where she had been awarded a prestigious fellowship to train in haute couture.

For my grandmother, sewing beautiful clothing was a gesture of resistance. It meant she retained her individuality. She was Rose: a brilliant seamstress, a good skier, an indifferent cook. Sewing was synonymous with survival. In Germany, an antisemitic boss hired her to make dresses, blouses, coats. The woman—whose every word snipped like scissors—couldn't deny the perfection of my grandmother's seams. Yes, she saw Oma as *a dirty Jew*. But my grandmother could work for cheap, and her fine embroidery commanded big prices. She was made to sit in the darkest corner of the shop, bent over a gown that twinkled with sequins, her face in shadow so that no one had to worry about Jewish hands contaminating their clothes.

Rose stayed in Stuttgart, until it became clear that remaining there would mean dying. While her passion was the thread and the needle, delicate beading like rows of glassy seeds planted in a silken field, she was politically astute enough to understood that her life meant nothing to the state. She persuaded her mother and siblings that it was time to leave. In 1936, unable to secure visas to enter the United States, the family emigrated instead to Honduras, where they had relatives.

Decades later in America, my Oma spoke an English stitched with the rough textures of her native German, as well as with the fine threads of Spanish she learned in her late twenties. When we visited the fabric store, we walked together down the narrow aisles and touched the rainbowed bolts of cotton. During these hours, she instructed me in how to cut on the bias, the best way to sew chiffon without snagging the silk, and how to know when a democracy is in danger.

Her lessons basted fashion to history. A hem was not merely a hem, but a story about statelessness, what people took with them when they fled their homes. A collar was more than a collar; it was a memory of her first years in San Pedro Sula, how my own mother struggled in Catholic school, the only Jewish child in every classroom. When Oma sewed me a shirt or a skirt, she took my measurements in a small book, her notes in a German scrawl of loops and knots, a language of displacement and loss.

61

I thought of Oma as I walked through the cavernous storage rooms of the Texas Fashion Collection at the University of North Texas, where I teach. The director and curator, Annette Becker, was showing me some of her favorite pieces. Like my grandmother, Becker clearly loved fabric, the thought and attention that go into making a fine piece of clothing, the meticulous stitches—like beautiful secrets—that are hidden on the inside of a garment.

For hours, we paced the aisles. Becker pulled from one of the racks a jacket designed to look like a mosaic floor in Rome. She held out a dress printed with butterflies and a matching silk chiffon cape bearing more wings so that, when the two parts were worn together, the insects seemed to flutter with air. On another hanger: a piece with thick layers of quilting. Prints in dazzling profusion. Mini dresses made of paper and meant to be worn just once.

Chanel suits in red and cream and black. Ball gowns, bridal gowns, furs, and feathers. A coat of *imperial sable* lined in *royal blue silk*.

Becker smiled as she pointed to a pair of swimming briefs designed by Jean Paul Gaultier. The nylon was decorated with a scene of women in blue and white, which is inspired by Mexican ceramics, she said. "To make the illustration readable, the briefs have to be really filled out,"[80] Becker observed, and I laughed at the bulge which was, indeed, prominent.

Near the end of our tour, she showed me a 2007 evening ensemble by Escada. "This dress was never meant to be worn," she explained. Each pin tuck was trimmed with bugle beads. She gestured toward a small area on the skirt. "Just this front panel of beading might have taken two full weeks of work." Later, when I read the description of the ensemble posted on the website, I saw that the prose couldn't convey the dress's magnificence, this uncanny, futuristic armor made of the most delicate materials:

> Gown of purple-gray pleated chiffon embellished with beads, sequins, and gems surrounding flat silver metal rectangles. Bodice is strapless with constructed bust and princess seams. Full-length skirt is heavily embellished with purple-gray feathers; lined in plum silk satin. . . . Vest of flat silver metal rectangles surrounded by beads, sequins, and gems trimmed and embellished with purple-gray feathers; lined in plum silk satin.[81]

No real body could wear a thing so fitted. Its skirt was too tight for walking. Its feathered train dragged heavy on the ground.

During my visit to the Texas Fashion Collection, I shot a video of the dress. And now, writing about the piece, I keep returning to its strange contrasts of hard and soft, the tension of metallic beading and airy feathers.[82] Entirely unwearable, this is clothing as art.

62

I love the canvases of John Singer Sargent for their lavish treatment of fashion in the Gilded Age. The artist's commissioned pictures of powerful socialites and prominent men manage to praise his subjects and to suggest that there's more here—these people are complex, powerful, perhaps not entirely deserving of our esteem. With paintings such as *Madame X* (Madame Pierre Gautreau) and *Lady Agnew of Lochnaw* (Gertrude Vernon Agnew), the artist offers us swaths of gleaming fabric, the one woman in black, the other in cream, both of their waists cinched impossibly small, their forms constrained by society's gaze.

Created between 1883 and 1884, *Madame X* provoked such controversy when it was first presented to the Parisian public that Sargent later repainted the strap of her dress, so that it no longer slipped from her shoulder but sat in its proper place. Still, even with that correction to her attire, *Madame X* remains a striking composition. Against the cloth's dark sheen, her neck, bodice, and uncovered arms seem vulnerable, the skin almost a pale purple. It's as if our eyes, passing over her body, might raise goosebumps there and cause her to shiver at our touchless touch. Scholar and curator Stephanie L. Herdrich writes that many viewers found the portrait "unflattering and eccentric."[83] To my eyes, the painting is utterly modern, Sargent's subject stylish and unashamed. While Madame Gautreau became a source of fascination "in society, . . . on the wall of the Salon, she was jeered." And sometimes a dress is more than dress. Herdrich emphasizes that *Madame X* and the fallen strap of her gown served as "a potent symbol of an upstart American who threatened to topple long-standing hierarchies in fashion, society, and national identity."[84]

Painted nearly ten years later, in 1892, *Lady Agnew of Lochnaw* offers no sultry provocations. This time, the woman doesn't stand for her portrait. Her head isn't turned to the side, revealing a sharpened profile. Lady Agnew leans back in a chair patterned with roses. Behind her hangs blue fabric, shimmering in a way that can only be silk. She resembles a birthday present tied with a lavender bow. Her bodice is trimmed in what looks like organza; her puffed sleeves are translucent too. The skin she shows is not seductive. But, despite the softness of the scene—all those delicate textiles suggesting a life of cushioned repose—Lady Agnew stares at the viewer, her expression direct and frank. She refuses to look away.

63

Novelist D. H. Lawrence once complained about Sargent's paintings. They were "nothing but yards and yards of satin from the most expensive shops, having some pretty head propped up on at the top," he grumbled. "The imagination is quite dead.[85] As much as I admire Lawrence's prose style, I don't agree with this assessment. Sargent's paintings do glisten with luxuriant layers of satin. The women's faces do perch, their eyes and smiles sometimes secondary to the marvelous confections of their gowns. But imagination is always visible in a painting by Sargent. His canvases are not photographic in their realism.

Take, for instance, *A Venetian Woman,* which was painted in 1882, the same year that Sargent completed *El Jaleo,* a sweeping scene that portrays the uproar of flamenco dance on a vast stretch of canvas. *El Jaleo* shows a woman. Her torso is feathered with shadow, one hand outstretched in an impossible arch, the other lifting her white skirt into dramatic, urgent folds. In the background sit the musicians and the waiting dancers. Fingers are caught mid-pluck of the string. Mouths open in a cry. Sargent's brush evokes the spin and shriek, shocks of black paint jagged against cream and little splashes of color. A red shawl. An unpeeled orange placed on the cane seat of a chair.

In canvases like *A Venetian Woman* and *El Jaleo,* a viewer can see how Sargent paints those he deems to be thrillingly *other*. The brushstrokes are loose, the poses of the models more relaxed than in his paintings of monied sirs and ladies. The clothing—Sargent always depicts fabric so attentively, with such awareness of social standing—seems less fitted to the figure, designed not for fancy dress balls but for work and movement. The model in *A Venetian Woman* is beautiful. She requires no flattering angles. She doesn't need a painter to raise her stature with his skillful draftsmanship. The shawl arranged over her shoulders has a spectacular, grapey hue, like wine spun into wool. She lifts her ruffled skirt, its butter-yellow hem, to reveal a narrow ankle, the shiny tip of a shoe.

64

Once, a few years ago, I went to an exhibit of handicrafts made in Venice. This is where I first saw Sargent's *A Venetian Woman,* her portrait hung among the displays of glass beads and delicate mosaics. Entering the gallery, I came across a clear vase from Murano. Circa 1880s or '90s, it was tall, the mouth and base rimmed in teal. Three transparent dolphins swam around the watery stem, and between each creature sat a chrysanthemum formed of opaque glass. I leaned toward the display case to study the small details, how the sea creatures' eyes bulged as if in surprise, their hungry, open mouths.

The vessel was nearly 150 years old. The rippling tails of the dolphins, which ended in sharp points, remained unchipped. I couldn't imagine the vase ever held a bouquet of roses. Its only duty was to be fine and breakable.

In a different case, I found a display of lace. According to a placard in the exhibit, a revival of Venetian glassmaking in the 1870s led to the return of other local crafts. My favorite piece was a long strip of rosettes embroidered on mesh, each bud slightly raised, a relief of flowers needled to a backdrop of latticed air. Hard to believe the threads had remained so clean, barely yellowed by the decades. The finished lace would have been attached to a collar or stitched to the wrist of a sleeve. It might have served as a handkerchief but not one to dab a wet brow with, never for wiping a nose. With its pallor and fragility, the lace was the material equivalent of a Murano goblet: entirely decorative, too fragile for use.

I couldn't feel any anger about the Murano glass or the strips of lace. I concede that these things were impractical. However frivolous the objects on display, their making took great skill; they remained works of pure artistry.

65

Recently, I watched a film about the twentieth-century photographer Lee Miller. In one of the early scenes, the main character tells her new lover that she's not frivolous. Miller insists she's not, with a stiff glance over her shoulder. At this point in the story, she has left behind her career as a fashion model and has begun shooting her own pictures for *Vogue*, often of other women gleaming in sleek corsets, their limbs glossy and golden.

The rest of the movie is a response to this accusation of frivolity. Miller becomes a war correspondent. She takes iconic shots inside combat zones across Europe and, later, she documents the atrocities of death camps like Buchenwald and Dachau. Her camera takes in the stacked corpses, uncanny piles of bones.

Most famously, her colleague David E. Scherman once snapped a picture of her seated naked in the tiled bathtub of Hitler's Munich apartment. Miller leans forward, one hand hidden, the other pressing a wet washcloth against her shoulder blade. On the right edge of the frame, there's a small plaster nude placed on a vanity. The sculpture looks vaguely classical; it resembles one of the pale-limbed, Aryan figures we might see in Leni Riefenstahl's film about the 1936 Berlin Olympics, *Olympia.* On the bathtub rim, at the left edge of the photograph, there's a small picture of the Führer himself, although by this point Hitler was dead in a bunker. Both the dictator and the tiny nude woman seem to stare at Miller, who sits at the center of the scene, perhaps because she is the one who has survived the destruction and now must wash herself of its stench. The artist Chris Wiley observes that this image would become an "apt visual metaphor for the end of the war."[86] The photograph was taken, Wiley writes, after a bleak day on which Miller's camera had witnessed dozens of horrors: "At Dachau, that morning, she had photographed piles of bodies in trucks and train cars, which had escaped incineration only because the camp had run out of fuel five days prior; skeletal prisoners still warehoused in their bare bunks, too weak and sick to celebrate their freedom; an S.S. guard, unjustly placid in death, floating in a canal."

Seated in the pale mouth of Hitler's bathtub, Miller doesn't smile. Her face is motionless, unlined. She looks up and off toward some object that lies beyond the boundary of the photograph. She stares at the recent past, I suspect, toward a courtyard where corpses are heaped on the ground and the living prisoners stand in the hard sunlight.

66

In the Year of Perfect Skin, I visited the dermatologist's office for my annual screening. The doctor's nose and lips were covered by a paper mask. But she had rubbed her eyelids with an elaborate, peacock-flourish of blue. Her liner curved upward like the tips of feathers slightly curled. With this small act of artistry, she asserted her individuality. She undid the concealment of the mask, which flattened every face, removing the expressiveness of a mouth, the identifying features of cheekbones and chin.

The doctor searched my body for signs of sickness—small marks that mean death—and, for a moment, I could barely breathe. I was certain she would find something terrible on me, a tiny brown dot on my forearm, a rough patch on the curve of my thigh.

67

Identifying frivolity is not as simple as dividing the world into the silly and the serious. For instance, we can't claim that all fashion is frivolous. A pair of Levi's blue jeans made from 100 percnt cotton that was woven in an American mill might be expected to get fifteen or twenty years of use. The heavy denim is weighted with practicality. I can imagine the jeans worn by a farmer or a student heading from the classroom to her part-time job.

68

On the other hand, a pale pink gown constructed in the style of an eighteenth-century court dress—all frills and puffy layers of pale tulle, a line of silk roses stitched across the bodice—feels like frivolity given (material) form.

69

And what about something like perfume? This thing composed of molecules is just as difficult to understand. We can't say that all fragrances are shallow adornments for the skin. A scent that has been produced in the German city of Cologne for more than two hundred years, 4711 has been marketed as "miracle water" and smells bracingly of citrus, lavender, and rosemary, notes almost medicinal in their sharpness.

70

Meanwhile, Guerlain's Shalimar was created in 1925, a century ago. Like 4711, it contains bergamot and other citrus fruits, but the notes float on a cloud of sweet vanilla and jasmine, tendrils of alluring incense. There is nothing curative about Shalimar, the perfume's name derived from that of a princess in an ancient love story. The two fragrances exist on a continuum, at one end the utility of 4711 and at the opposite end the romance of Shalimar.

So, this is the challenge of understanding the frivolous, that it exists at one extreme of the spectrum while at the other resides the serious:

Frivolous ________________________________ Serious

For instance, daydreams are frivolous because they're fantasies, distractions from the hard duties of adulthood. But the dreams we have at night are serious; they offer us ciphered insights into what we most desire. False eyelashes are frivolous. False teeth are not.

More than ten years ago, Victor Wong, the founder and creative director of Zoologist Perfumes, left the video game industry to start a company that produces a line of scents inspired by creatures from the animal kingdom. Bee has notes of royal jelly, ginger syrup, and orange flower. Chipmunk skitters with whiffs of hazelnut, nutmeg, and chamomile. Each bottle is decorated with a black-and-white illustration of an animal posing for its portrait, a cow dressed as a milkmaid, a harvest mouse outfitted like a country squire, a hummingbird attired in an elegant gown.

Over email, I ask Wong how he first fell in love with perfume. He tells me it was a set of fancy hotel toiletries that led to his interest in scent: "I discovered there's a universe of niche perfumes and began seeking out different interesting fragrances to smell, learning about perfume notes, reading books and blogs on them, and participating in social media discussions dedicated to perfumes."[87] After entering the world of fragrance, falling down "the rabbit hole," as he calls it, Wong didn't immediately leave behind his day job. He founded Zoologist Perfumes but treated the business as a "serious hobby," until balancing the two careers became unfeasible.

Zoologist Perfumes are playful and joyous. But each perfume also contains a serious element; often it's an individual note, like the black ink accord in Squid or the resins in Moth. Wong believes that the fun and serious can coexist. He doesn't worry about justifying his love of fragrance to others. "Everyone has their own indulgence and reasons and it's futile to explain and persuade others why it's worthwhile," he observes. "A good perfume is like a good book, it's more rewarding to read it yourself; telling someone who doesn't read that it's a good book probably means very little."

I am such an admirer of Zoologist Perfumes that I once sent fan letter to Victor and asked if we could collaborate. He suggested I create a poem for one of Zoologist's forthcoming scents, Rabbit. This is the sonnet I wrote:

> Tonight, the air is green with clover, hay,
> and little clumps of grasses on the breeze,
> unsettled dirt, the dusty mysteries
> of rabbits tunneling the dark. They stray
> into the meadow, sniff the wind—bouquet
> of violets. They hop in twos and threes,
> their shadows cotton-tailed. Or else they freeze
> when something feathered screeches far away,
> unmoving, tufted stones. But now the night
> goes soft and jasmine-sweet again. A scent
> of petals presses to their fur. There's fruit
> to eat. There is the skittering delight
> of digging into earth, the sediment
> of dreams perfumed with carrot-top and root.[88]

Someone who buys a bottle of Rabbit will find my poem printed on the packaging, above a list of notes, which include apple, clover flower, and biscuit. When I drafted the sonnet, I often paused to sniff my wrist, a sample of Rabbit sprayed at my pulse, so that the perfume drifted toward my nose in little threads of sweet and spice. It was one of the most pleasurable experiences of writing I've ever had. I felt unburdened. My task was simply to find language that evoked the fragrance's joy, its lightness in the air.

"Rabbit" is a Petrarchan sonnet. I picked the form for practical reasons; I knew that a sonnet's boxy shape—those 14 lines of iambic pentameter—would fit the narrow frame of the perfume bottle's packaging. I have written many sonnets in my career, poems that have explored the form's traditional and more serious territories: faith, death, desire. But, as any sonneteer knows, despite its rigid appearance on the page, this is the most flexible of fixed forms. It is a tiny container of words. It is roomy enough to hold humor and wit, jubilant leaps of thought. It can even serve a practical purpose: to market a vial of green scent.

As I wrote my scented sonnet, I remembered a favorite novel from childhood, Richard Adams's *Watership Down,* which tells the story of a group of displaced rabbits in search of a new home, a land of milk thistle and honey. It sounds silly—a furred odyssey. The rabbit characters speak their own language, called Lapine. They sing bunny songs. They recount creation myths to explain what terrifies them most, the snap of a twig in the forest, a shadowy bird of prey briefly darkening the moon.

In one story, we learn how rabbits got their long hind legs and fluffy tails. Lord Frith, the sun-god, accuses the rabbit trickster El-ahrairah of pride. He punishes the rabbit with a cast of predators, including dogs, cats, weasels, and hawks. But, in return for such terror, Frith grants El-ahrairah's people speed and intelligence: "All the world will be your enemy, Prince with a Thousand Enemies, and whenever they catch you, they will kill you. But first they must catch you, digger, listener, runner, prince with the swift warning. Be cunning and full of tricks and your people shall never be destroyed."[89]

The writer Madeline Miller, whose best-selling novels recount or reinvent classical Greek myths, says of *Watership Down*:

> Adams keeps the stakes from the great epics: war, loss, death, and the powerful threads of community and personal courage, but instead of imagining them on a grand stage, he sets them, with utter seriousness, in the English countryside among ordinary bunnies. This could feel absurd, but it doesn't, because as Adams understands, courage is even more thrilling when you aren't half-immortal, when you don't have ichor in your veins, when you're a prey animal who has a thousand enemies trying to eat you every hour of every day. True epic, Adams shows us, isn't what gods do, but what underdogs do, in a world where there are no gods to help them.[90]

Watership Down is full of terror. Rabbits are gassed to death in a warren. They are clawed and bitten by their peers. They are strangled in a snare-wire trap. Although rabbits are adorable creatures, Adams shows readers that these animals' lives should be taken seriously, the stories they tell themselves a way of surviving in this fanged, devouring world.

72

At some point during the Year of Perfect Skin, I stopped wearing perfume. Many of us were shut in our houses then. My own life was three bedrooms and two baths, some windows looking out onto a row of beige houses, a little fenced-in lawn. In summer, the north Texas grass scorched yellow. Later, in the cold months, the pavement sometimes darkened as though wet, last night's glaze of dew frozen over, although the weather never stayed icy for very long.

For more than a decade, scent had been a passion. I called it one of my great loves. I had published books about it, given lectures, taught classes on how to soak one's poems in the thick aromas of memory, the dark smoke of a campfire, a grandmother's lilac and peppermint, the tangy sweat of gym class. But during the first months of the pandemic, I couldn't imagine my skin smelling of anything but its own nervousness.

It wasn't that I lost my sense of smell, the way so many people did during that time. One of the side effects of the virus could be anosmia. Suddenly, there were dozens of articles written by people—often those formerly indifferent to the misty powers of smell—who had discovered that the world becomes eerie when bleached of fragrance. People complained about their food. Without scent, a bite of spaghetti bolognese turned to strands of lumpen cardboard in the mouth. Oranges, lemons became nothing more than sharp liquids that stung the tongue.

I hadn't lost my sense of smell. But I feared my own skin. One of the pleasures of wearing perfume is how it alters over a day. A great fragrance moves through unexpected stages, one moment a sprig of neroli, the next, a purple field of irises and, finally, oakmoss and leather, a smoothed piece of sandalwood. To wear perfume is to be reminded of time, that it passes, that we fade, that we eventually disappear.

During those early months, I was afraid of all the things I couldn't see. Infection floated like a vapor, its residue left on polished surfaces. I had always loved that perfume was potent in its invisibility. It was like a fog that settled on the body, wafting outward to fill the corners of a room, following the wearer like a twisting shadow.

In the vocabulary of perfumes, collectors of scent speak about the trail that a fragrance leaves behind. Sillage. It's French for the wake of a ship, the way a vessel creates a path of movement as it cuts through water. A perfume with magnificent sillage trails after us, almost palpable in its presence, thick and velvety.

Sillage is not so much perceived by the wearer as it is by others in a room. Perhaps, this is because we so often struggle to turn back and consider the liquid path we've just taken.

And what is the sillage of trauma? How does it follow us?

73

There was a time my marriage nearly ended. We came close to shattering like a glass bottle dropped on a tile floor.

In the months after—as I tried to find a way back to my husband, stepping slowly toward him through the breakage—I often felt like I stood at a great distance from my body. It was delicate and placed on a high shelf that I couldn't (or didn't want to) reach.

To distract myself from the problems of love, I began to read about scent. How difficult it was, I realized, to make something so ephemeral concrete. Our language is impoverished when it comes to words for smell. It's not enough to say that a fragrance is *strong* or *weak*. *Pretty* or *ugly*.

Memorable or *forgettable*. Instead, to convey the experience of encountering an odor, the writer must craft a figurative language, one that begins with sight and sound, taste and texture. Scent resists being captured in words. It wants to dissipate. It wants to fade faster than a writer can explain its volatility, the aldehydes and notes of citrus that vanish almost as soon as they're sprayed on skin.

How difficult it was too, I realized, to write about this moment in a marriage. I couldn't find the right words for speaking about our near dissolution. We did not end our marriage or separate, but something had been divided. The feelings that had bound us together like molecules were being split apart into their separate, distant atoms.

There is the idiom: to come to one's senses. It means: to return to logical thought after a time of unreason. I came to my senses by falling excessively, expensively in love with perfumes and with olfaction itself. In the early days of my new passion, I would pull my wrist to my nose, drag my nostrils across the blue-lined veins, the natural and the synthetic colliding deep within my brain.

I discovered the delights of sampling: the ability to smell ten perfumes, those tiny vials of surprise, each one asking a question. *Could you love me? Will you love me?* Some samples suggested enormous beauty—a burst of orange blossoms, perhaps, or a flood of roses. Untested, they seemed to offer just what I was looking for. But then, when I dabbed one on my wrist, the perfume surprised with horror. I went searching for the ideal vanilla. But every vial offered me disgust. One scent reeked of mold and wet tobacco, the sweaty thighs of cigar-rollers. Another was mostly dust in a library filled with decomposing books. *Do you love me?* they asked. No, I could never.

In grief or trauma, we are divorced from ourselves. It is easier to forget limbs and limbic system than to remain connected to so much pain. But, after a few weeks, and then a year, all these aromas brought me back. Testing the terrible alongside the exquisite allowed me to slowly reach toward myself. I no longer sat on a high, dusty shelf. And this was how I eventually decided I could love someone else again, could love my husband, who had handled that glass bottle so clumsily. I found that I could forgive him for fumbling the faceted stopper of our marriage.

74

A long time ago, when I first began to write about my passion for perfume, I tried to explain why one should care about something so ephemeral. What reason to adore the cool mists of vetiver? The violet's furred touch?

"In a dark time, I am in love with something frivolous," I say on the opening page of a book.[91] Later, I admit, "I can't explain away my frivolity."[92]

That's the thing about some forms of pleasure—Americans call them "guilty."[93] We call others "innocent." And because ours is a country founded in part by Puritans, we seat our delights in a courtroom and announce our verdicts with a loud, hammering gavel.

75

Sometimes I imagine living in Tuscany, walking roads lined with the long shadows of cypress trees. Or maybe I should return to Vicenza, where I was born, a city famous for its carved arches and colonnades.

The Italians have an expression, *la dolce far niente*. Pleasant idleness. The sweetness of doing nothing. The French speak of *l'art de ne rien faire*; they make an art form out of inactivity.

In English, we have words like *sloth*, *indolence*, *lethargy*. Doing nothing is neither delicious nor artful. To sit at a café all day, sipping a shot of espresso or a glass of something red—every passerby an opportunity for eavesdropping—is understood as laziness. Shiftlessness is a great moral failing and an indication of weak character.

Americans are the people of *if you have time to lean, you have time to clean*. All twenty-six letters of the English alphabet are contained in the sentence *The quick brown fox jumps over the lazy dog*. Americans believe time is a thing that can be wasted; like money, time is finite. One can be a master of slack. It is possible to be lazy down to one's bones. Thumbs should not be twiddled. Feet should not be dragged. Hands should never idle, or they risk becoming tools of the devil.

76

In an interview with the *Paris Review*, acclaimed French playwright and novelist Yasmina Reza explains why she seeks out frivolity in her work:

> I find frivolousness to be very deep. The frivolous is the foam that floats over the depths. Human drama doesn't consist of big tragic incidents. Naturally, they happen in the course of a life—but for the most part, it's full of small

> details, minor scrapes, wrinkles, micro-events, that together make up the struggle of being. Infinitely more than losing one's mother at eight. That's what I'm interested in most, what I track down is how the fabric of a life wears out, how it hurts, how it's irrational, through tiny details that might seem trifles. I choose to pick at what seems most irrelevant, most superficial, most unfit to dig into, and I dig into it—that's how I write.[94]

Reza's play *God of Carnage* exemplifies this approach. She uses frivolous dialogue to examine two civilized couples. *God of Carnage* demonstrates how easily politeness may be scraped away to reveal the savagery of human nature, our violence and brutality barely suppressed by small talk, all those conventions of polite society. Over the course of the play, the couples attempt to resolve a conflict between their young sons—one boy having assaulted the other—but only manage to descend into their own vicious squabbles about gender, class, and race. Much of the superficial conversation centers on a dessert that one of the wives serves at the meeting:

> *Michael:* So, clafouti, is it a cake or a tart? Serious question. I was just thinking in the kitchen, Linzertorte, for example, is that a tart? Come on, come on, you can't leave that one little slice.
>
> *Veronica:* Clafouti is a cake. The pastry's not rolled out, it's mixed in with the fruit.
>
> *Alan:* You really are a cook.
>
> *Veronica:* I love it. The thing about cooking is you have to love it. In my opinion, it's only the classic tart, that's to say on a pastry base, that deserves to be called a tart.[95]

Clafouti is a traditional French dessert, simple but hard to perfect. It's sometimes eaten for breakfast but is delicious at the end of a meal too. In *God of Carnage,* the clafouti becomes a shorthand for all the things we do and say to avoid conflict, especially when we're communicating with strangers. Each time the conversation edges toward ugliness, one of the four characters returns to that clafouti. Unfortunately, the dessert itself leads to the most shocking moments in the piece, when the character Annette vomits—what's described as a "*brutal and catastrophic spray*"—across the set.[96] The clafouti's cloying sweetness disgusts her. And it's her violent nausea that finally allows the characters to speak coarsely and cruelly; they can be frank with one another. The spewing of frivolity allows the four people on stage to reveal their barbarousness, the violence of Annette's regurgitation permitting all of them to hurl violent, sickening words.

77

The modest macaroon tastes like rebellion in Henrik Ibsen's famous portrait of a Norwegian housewife, *A Doll's House.* Within the first two pages of the play, the stage instructions describe Nora pulling a bag of cookies from her pocket. She eats a few. And, almost as soon as her husband enters, he begins quizzing her about what she bought, calling her his "spending bird" and asking, "Is frivolity out for a stroll again?"[97]

And then there's this exchange:

> *Helmer [wags a stern finger]*: My sweet-tooth wouldn't perhaps have been on the rampage in town today?

Nora: No, how can you think such a thing.
Helmer: Did my sweet-tooth really not make a detour into the confectioner's?
Nora: No, I assure you, Torvald—
Helmer: Not nibbled at a little jam?
Nora: No, absolutely not.
Helmer: Not even gnawed a macaroon or two?[98]

Later, Nora presses macaroons into the mouths of two visitors to the house before taking several more for herself. Eating a cookie is her miniature act of insurrection. Each time she bites into another macaroon, Nora chews at the gritty constraints of her life: Torvald and his nagging control, her lack of financial freedom, the confinement of domesticity.

78

During the great confrontation at the end of the play, when Nora realizes the truth about her marriage—that it is sweet and empty, its own sort of frivolous concoction—she breaks with Torvald. "In eight whole years—no, more—ever since our first meeting, we've never exchanged a serious word about serious things."[99] Their life together was a confection that resembled love, like a piece of pink fondant molded into the shape of a rosebud.

Nora is, as she explains to her husband, a doll who has spent her days being posed in miniature houses, first her father's home and then later her husband's. The macaroon is the perfect food for dolls. It's a tiny, dense cookie, too sweet, a cloying dessert that causes tooth decay.

79

And what of another cookie? Hamantaschen are associated with story of Purim. According to the biblical tale, Queen Esther saves her people from destruction at the hands of the Persian court official Haman. In the Jewish calendar, Purim is one of the great celebratory moments. It's a holiday that revels in frivolous things. Happiness becomes the only possible response to near catastrophe.

I'm reminded of a treasured joke. It comes from the idea that many Jewish holidays can be reduced to the assertion *They tried to kill us. They failed. Let's eat.*

Every Purim, Jews acknowledge how close and how often we have come to annihilation. We make noise and laugh as a way of pushing back our fears. We blot out a tyrant's name. Comedy is the relief from tragedy, the reprieve from approaching disaster, the response to an almost massacre.

Hamantaschen are dense shortbread cookies in the shape of Hamman's three-cornered hat. They're often filled with poppyseeds or apricot jam, overflowingly sweet. Purim asks, *What else should we consume but this kind of sugar and fat, when we have stood so close to cataclysm?*

Maybe the answer to destruction—that Esther saves us with her intelligence and bravery—must be frivolity, raucous celebration, the wild rebellion of joy.

80

During the worst moments of the global pandemic, it seemed like everyone I knew had found a hobby. My husband learned how to make mosaics. He laid chips of glass in the grooves and surfaces of old hunks of metal. He kept breaking and repairing, the mosaic his effort to fix what was fractured during those months and years. A friend taught himself to bake bread. He scored the top of each loaf, becoming so adept with the knife that he could pattern the dough with a sheaf of wheat or an intricate symmetry of lines. Meanwhile, I wove scarves on a tabletop loom. I refined my recipe for seafood paella.

These diversions consumed time. Locked in our houses, no longer commuting to work or school, we had too many spare hours. In her book *Wintering: The Power of Rest and Retreat in Difficult Times,* Katherine May discusses the hard moments in our lives when we are forced into a condition that resembles winter, made to retreat into ourselves after a death or sickness or sudden change: "Once we stop wishing it were summer, winter can be a glorious season in which the world takes on a sparse beauty and even the pavements sparkle. It's a time for reflection and recuperation, for putting your house in order."[100] And that's what the pandemic was—a long wintering, when many of us had no choice but to curl together in our dens like furred animals.

Our hobbies were not, in fact, frivolous. My husband's mosaics sat in the garden, brilliant colors glinting from behind the leaves of the desert willow or the Texas sage. My scarves warmed our necks all winter. My paella fed us. And my friend's sourdough tasted delicious. His bread communicated a longing for comfort, that fundamental craving for something warm, to make deliciousness out of a few simple ingredients. Flour. Salt. Yeast.

I had the Year of Perfect Skin. Others had the Year of Rosebushes, the Year of Model Airplanes, the Year of

Crochet. If we scratch the surface of most frivolities, we find need underneath, a longing to be safe or adored or a little less afraid.

81

In her essay "The Year That Skin Care Became a Coping Mechanism," writer Jia Tolentino explains why she developed a beauty regimen in her late twenties. Horrified by the policies of a certain American president, she chooses to focus on beautification instead, not to look young forever but as a small gesture of political resistance. "Skin seemed like a nice controllable project," she muses, before confessing, "As it turned out, it both was and was not."[101]

For Tolentino, the pursuit of skin's perfection is a way of accepting that a flawless face is as precarious as this moment in which we live. "I wonder if women my age are less afraid of looking older than we are of the possibility that there will be no functional world to look old in." Perfect skin becomes, then, a thin barrier against "climate destruction and violent nationalism."

I suppose Tolentino's reasons for layering collagens and essences make as much sense as do mine. When she purchases costly creams, she questions whether she is "buying skin care or a psychological safety blanket." In the Year of Perfect Skin, I wanted to believe that every time I steamed my pores or coated myself in a thick clay mask—my face an uncanny sheath of gray—I was keeping the pandemic far away. No virus could touch me. Nothing could seep inside.

82

Blaise Pascal, the seventeenth-century polymath, would likely have understood Tolentino's impulse to use skin care as a distraction from the bleakness of the quotidian. In his *Pensées*—a collection of aphorisms and brief meditations—the philosopher examines the reasons we look away from the hollowness of daily life:

> Anyone who does not see the vanity of the world is very vain himself. So who does not see it, apart from young people whose lives are all noise, diversions, and thoughts for the future?
>
> But take away their diversion and you will see them bored to extinction. Then they feel their nullity without recognizing it, for nothing could be more wretched than to be intolerably depressed as soon as one is reduced to introspection with no means of diversion.[102]

In my yellowed copy of the *Pensées*, I discover some marginalia from my college days. Beside this passage, I had scribbled one word in pencil: *Ouch!* Even at twenty, I understood that Pascal was right, at least about me and my need for diversion.

As Pascal sees it, a diversion is what causes us to forget our own insignificance and weakness. We take up "gambling, hunting, some absorbing show," and for a little while we stop ruminating.[103] Here are echoes of Montaigne's description of vanity: "the sea grows troubled and turbulent when it is tossed back on itself."[104] Diversion allows the ocean to look away from its waves. The sea can go on splashing without ever having to consider its own currents.

Pascal writes that "the sole cause of man's happiness is that he does not know how to stay quietly in his room."[105] But what is the alternative to seeking out diversion? If we don't occupy our time with frivolities, then we're forced to face bleak observations such as this one: "The eternal silence of these infinite spaces fills me with dread."[106] Endless spaces are indeed terrifying—that hugeness of the universe, that vast, starry indifference to our little selves. What could be scarier?

The philosopher observes that "the parrot wipes its beak although it is clean."[107] I take this to mean that an avian of brilliant plumage needs a pastime to endure its green surroundings. The bird swipes a wing across its beak. This gesture diverts the animal from the unnerving silence of the trees and the vines that tangle like ropes. It pretends to brush away some speck of dirt, because it too knows the squawking dread of these endless spaces.[108]

83

The bird wipes its beak. The bee stands in the center of a rose. The dog rests its face on a carpet.

In the great hierarchy of subjects to be painted, dogs rank above a vaseful of tulips. They rank below a scene of mountains veiled in weather. They are also lesser than a woman darning socks, also a portrait of a pope in all his velvets, also the picture of a famous lady kneeling before the execution block, a strip of satin covering her eyes. In other words, canines are useful creatures for the artist to study, but they are not seen as figures worthy of important art. Nonetheless, the sight of a dog reproduced in oils may comfort a viewer, much as a hand is reassured when it strokes the silk of a spaniel's ear.

It is hard for an artist to show a dog's motions. I would argue that the best depiction can be found in a painting from 1912, Giacoma Balla's *Dynamism of a Dog on a Leash*. Balla has captured how the dachshund's legs and tail appear to multiply into dozens of appendages, speed communicated in the blur of its body. *Dynamism* is especially impressive given how difficult it is to represent on canvas the waggle-tail that means hello, the snoot dragged along the ground in search of scent, the royal hunting hound who rolls in the grass as a way of getting at an itch. It's difficult too to draw a canine yawning; the long tongue curls down then up, an acrobatic glistening, before the pink loops back into the mouth again. Stilled on canvas, most dogs resemble animals stuffed.

Even a dog asleep resists the efforts of the painter. Dozing is not the same as immobility. On leaning close, it's possible to observe twitches or snuffles. The sleeping mutt continues to inhale pungent news of the night. It smells a plate of cookies rooms away, an uncapped pen, an opened door fanning in the cut-grass smell, a neighbor's garbage can parked at the curb, and the spray of canine messages left on trees and hydrants and fences down the street.

There's something to be said for the artist who depicts, not the circle of mastiff gamblers playing cards at a green table, but a dog in sleek repose. Most of the time, the animal will turn out taxidermied on the canvas, stiff-limbed and mounted in its place. But occasionally, brushwork loosens into movement, and the dog appears to breathe.

In many of Mary Cassatt's paintings and drawings, the presence of a small canine adds a humorous, bourgeois element to her compositions. See, for example, *Little Girl in a Blue Armchair* from 1878. A child reclines in a room that is filled, inexplicably, with bright blue armchairs and a blue settee, all the furniture marshmallow-plump and adorned with a meadow of flowers. There's a wall of gauzy windows at the back of the room, but there is no door. No way of getting out. Certainly, the girl is alive and prodigiously jaded. She leans back in her white petticoat, a tartan bow in her hair and more plaid on her skirt and her socks. But the dog is the real achievement here. It's some kind of black and brown terrier. Tufted ears. And look at the eyes, which are pinched shut in concentrated sleep. The dog dreams on, while the girl twists in her seat, her face mischievous, a naughty smile about to form.

About Cassatt's handling of domestic scenes such as the one depicted in *Little Girl in a Blue Armchair*, art historian Griselda Pollock writes:

> Cassatt formally studied the gestures of the labour peculiar to these spaces: be it the creative work of the bourgeoisie, such as embroidery or tapestry, or that of nursemaids bathing, comforting, playing with, and teaching, children. As an artist always preoccupied by the compositional challenge of bodies in space, Cassatt was also fascinated by generational difference. This meant the close study of the peculiarities of the unformed, fleshy child body versus the socially formed gestures and learned postures [of] adult women of different classes.
>
> Cassatt's formal study of child/adult interactions belongs, therefore, to the later 19th-century cultural moment when the child and the adolescent appeared as objects of both psychological inquiry and literary

> exploration. . . . We do Cassatt's paintings a deep injustice by collapsing them into the premodern iconography of 'mother and child'. Recognizing her novel and intensely formal explorations of the emerging subjectivity of the child and her/his socialization in relationship to adults, we can also discern appreciate the symbolist interest in psycho-social complexities shared with modernist writers and thinkers.[109]

So, what might the snoozing terrier represent? What psychosocial complexity can be read in its body, that it sleeps so easily as the girl sighs with boredom, her body cushioned on a blue-patterned field? The dog's indifference tells us this little girl will grow up to be a woman trapped in plump and pillowed rooms. She will always be dressed exquisitely. She will wear bows. Her hats will resemble the precarious tiers of wedding cakes.

84

Writing about dogs is almost as difficult as painting them. When I try to describe Argos, my first dog, words often harden on the computer screen. I came closest once, in explaining his death. In a book-length essay, I wrote that I knew it was time to put him to sleep when the wind kept knocking him over. It was early February. We stood on a hillside near my parents' house, and the breeze shoved against his wheat-gold fur. He was so thin—starving, really—that it took barely a breath to push him to the dirt.

Now, if I talk about my dogs, Lola and Bandit the Bedlington terriers, I search for the right shade of gray to name their fur. Stone gray. The gray of certain sidewalks. A silvered light. Small and fuzzy, they are among the frivolous breeds. They resemble sheep. *Lambs from outer space,* I call them. And while Bedlington terriers were once bred to hunt badgers in a chilly, English mining town, Lola and Bandit have never dug in the earth for any kind of creature. They use their tense jaws to tear apart a squeaky dragon or to murder a stuffed bear.

The poet Mark Doty once told me that Lola *was an ethereal cloud of dog.* He said that she had *a contemplative soul.* Doty writes exquisitely of his own dogs in *Dog Years,* a memoir about losing his partner to AIDS and the griefs that came after. "Most stories about dogs are narrated to other people," he says, "as we go on articulating the tales of our animals' lives, in order to bring their otherwise incomprehensible experience into the more orderly world of speech."[110] In *Dog Years,* Doty acknowledges the difficulty of talking about these creatures we love:

> Of course, listening to stories about other people's pets is perilous, like listening to the recitation of dreams. Such reports may be full of charm for the dreamer, but for the poor listener they're usually fatally dull. The dreamer has no distance from the spell of the dream, and cannot say just how it mattered so, and the language mostly fails to capture the deeply interior character of dreams anyway.[111]

I think Doty is right. Dogs are dreams that possess us too briefly. As I write this, Bandit is dying of cancer. By the time this book is published eighteen months from now, he will be dead. Some nights I watch Bandit's sturdy shadow in the dark. His profile swivels toward one corner of the room then another as if he were looking for death, which is a thing that skitters with tiny paws along the baseboards.

And today, exhausted from standing, he lay down in the backyard beside an orange rock, his body partly shadowed by the stone. I know pain will overtake his love of walking our neighborhood or of gripping a tennis ball in his mouth when it's time for dinner. Maybe as soon as a few days from now, the pain will be larger than those eastern bluebirds whose iridescent wings he loves to study, a flock of feathers arcing over the fence and streaking up toward the late afternoon of the sky.

Doty writes that "love for a wordless creature, once it takes hold, is an enchantment, and the enchanted speak, famously, in private mutterings, cryptic riddles, or gibberish."[112] But occasionally—woof-woofing or wheezing, snorting or snoring, big bellied after a meal and the beard wet with water—a dog leaps in language. A dog bites at its tail to offer the writer an image of want, longing circled on itself. A dog permits its chin to be scratched, because the writer needs an image of happiness on both sides, both the scratcher and the scratchee languid and fur-warm in one another's company.

85

I like to watch videos on the internet in which a parent surprises a child with a puppy. Usually, the dog is a birthday present. Sometimes the recipient is a teenager. Or maybe an old man has just lost his golden retriever of fifteen years. He's leaning back in his recliner, when he's approached by a cell phone already filming the scene.

Inevitably, the videos end with weeping. "Can I keep it," a little boy sobs as he holds the happy, wagging lump and cries into the puppy's side, its pale puff of fur.

Puppies are round. Their bodies squish when cuddled. Their tails, not yet elongated, are fuzzy triangles that move back and forth like joyful metronomes.

These videos are often captioned with symbols: a row of red hearts, a cartoon face dominated by oversized eyes that glisten, made gigantic with tears.

We don't deserve dogs, a stranger observes in the comments. *Why am I crying now,* someone else asks. *I'm not crying—you're crying,* another person types.

When I see the child clasping the new puppy, how he presses his face into the pink belly, I think about what's known as cute aggression. We see something so adorable that we want to taste it. The baby is practically edible, its toes like pale gumdrops, its elbows and knees squishy as rounds of yeasty dough.

Cute aggression is thought to be a response to intensely positive feelings. When we encounter something too adorable—a striped kitten so small she fits in the palm of a hand—the mind copes with such overwhelming sweetness by pushing back on itself, by replacing pleasure with the impulse to devour. You see? There is something that frightens us in the frivolous wriggling of a puppy.

86

What else frightens us? Loneliness, I think.

The romance novel, although it is derided as a frivolous literary genre, reassures readers. *You will find love. You won't be alone forever.* Romance novels are formulaic and therefore comforting; their narrative shape does not surprise. The book must begin with two people meeting adorably. The pair have chemistry. They spark like stone against steel. Then, the lovers face a conflict that could mean the collapse of everything between them. But, Reader, don't worry, because all ends well! The lovers embrace. *I love you, I love you,* they say in a tumble, a quick tearing off of clothes.

Romance novels tell us that a union of bodies can also mean a union of souls. They soothe with their assurances that sex can be good every time. Orgasms don't have to be elusive; pleasure is not an undiscovered country. Most significantly, these books promise that we can find friendship, love, everything we need in one person.

Throughout my childhood, I watched my Oma—my mother's mother—reading Harlequin romances. She practiced her English-language comprehension in the dime-store pages of those books. On every cover, there was heaving cleavage and a muscled torso. Sometimes the lovers wore costumes from another century. Occasionally, they were a modern pair, dressed in denim or leaning against the slick, red contours of a convertible. Their bodies were always sketched in thick, lustful brushstrokes.

Oma was not ashamed of her reading habits. She didn't hide her novels. She would sit in the living room, zipped up in a quilted housecoat, a crumpled Kleenex pushed up into the pink tunnel of one sleeve. I liked to watch her read, her quiet turning of the pages, a cup of tea or a few hard candies on the table beside her. There was no Hitler in her romance novels. No Nuremberg Laws. No Germany of the 1930s. Only desire and love existed for her during those hours.

87

Like the romance novel, the rom-com is plotted around a charming first encounter—what's known as the meet-cute—followed by other interactions that inevitably lead the beautiful, white-toothed protagonists toward one another. It's best if the film is cast with charismatic stars. It's particularly marketable if the story is set in a handsome locale, in Paris perhaps or near the Mediterranean Sea, a coastline with miles of pale sand. The costumes should be pretty, although at some point a dress will tear or a glass of wine will stain a shirt. Usually, the movie ends with a kiss, and the camera pushes in until we're close enough to smell the lovers, the salt of their sweat.

But in between that initial contact and that final admission of true love, something interferes. There's a misunderstanding, an old flame, events that are slapstick or raunchy. The two leads must each have a best friend offering advice on the telephone. Maybe there is a makeover. Maybe there's a montage. What matters is the obstacle to love; this is what makes us squirm in our seats. We eat the popcorn. We whisper together and laugh at the jokes. Much as we know how all this must end, we worry nonetheless, *will they or won't they.* As Lysander observes in *A Midsummer Night's Dream,* "The course of true love never did run smooth."[113] Desire is a winding river, and sometimes the lovers lose their balance on the wet banks and tumble into the shallows.

A friend of mine, a Renaissance scholar, tells me that *comedy is about the destitution of the human body.* In a rom-com, even when the film's rating in PG-13, the lovers are betrayed by what their bodies most want: to be fitted together intimately like two halves of a broken vase. This longing for union embarrasses the protagonists. Love reminds us that our hearts—although they beat inside our chests—act frequently in defiance. In a rom-com, the mind and the body are in conflict. "Lord, what fools these mortals be!" exclaims the naughty sprite Puck in the third act of *A Midsummer Night's Dreams,* but he could be talking about any pair of lovers in any almost any romantic comedy. [114]

In *Pursuits of Happiness: The Hollywood Comedy of Remarriage,* philosopher Stanley Cavell writes about the rom-coms of the 1930s and '40s, focusing on those in which a couple fall back in love after being divided (usually by divorce), movies like *Adam's Rib* and *The Philadelphia Story.* He argues that "the genre of remarriage is an inheritor of the preoccupations and discoveries of Shakespearean romantic comedy."[115] It's a bold claim, and he acknowledges the risk of his thesis. "I am not insensible, whatever defenses I may deploy, of an avenue of outrageousness in considering Hollywood films in the light, from time to time, of major works of thought," he writes.[116] "In subjecting these films to the same burden of interpretation that I expect any text to carry that I value as highly, I am aware that there are those for whom such an enterprise must from the start appear misguided, those who are satisfied that they know what film is, that it is, for example, a commodity like any other, or a visual medium of popular entertainment."[117]

Cavell recognizes that readers may be shocked to see frivolous entertainment analyzed in such a scholarly fashion. But what makes *Pursuits of Happiness* so rare is the philosopher's passion for frivolity, his belief that romantic comedies can teach us about our ourselves, our thoughts about love divided and love reunited. He writes that "to examine and defend my interest in these films is to examine and defend my interest in my own experience, in the moments and passages of my life I have spent with them."[118] I do much the same in these pages. To explore my interest in frivolity is to examine and defend the lightest parts of myself, the soul as an ice cream sundae topped with a spray of rainbow sprinkles.

88

One of my favorite rom-coms, *When Harry Met Sally*, is not about remarriage but, instead, enacts the trope of friends-to-lovers, the titular characters slowly realizing over the course of the film that they love and desire one another. We watch years of friendship. During that time, Harry and Sally change haircuts, jobs, sexual partners, but their connection remains constant, their banter witty, and their chemistry obvious to everyone else.

When Harry Met Sally was panned in the *New York Times* after its release in 1989, a critic observing that "Harry and Sally are defined by their witty, epigrammatic dialogue and so never become more than types."[119] Audiences seemed to disagree, and the movie quickly became part of the American rom-com canon. In her introduction to the screenplay, Nora Ephron explains that the film did not begin as an investigation of "whether men and women could be friends. The movie was instead a way for me to write about being single—about the difficult, frustrating, awful, funny search for happiness in an American city where the primary emotion is unrequited love."[120] And this is what makes *When Harry Met Sally* so effective, that it dramatizes the terrible specifics of what it's like to date, all those isolating things people do in the bedroom and outside of it as they search for the soul's companion.

Throughout *When Harry Met Sally*, we move back and forth between the story of our protagonists and brief interviews with couples explaining how they first met. Each pair sits close together on the matched cushions of a small sofa (a love seat, because this is a film about love, after all). Sometimes they interrupt one another. Sometimes one speaks while the other makes a knowing expression at the camera. The meetings happen by chance—in a cafeteria, in an elevator at the Ambassador Hotel, at a summer camp. Love is an accident, the interviews seem to imply. We don't earn it or do anything to deserve being saved from our solitude. Love occurs, and we are fortunate when it favors us.

At the end of the movie, we finally see Harry and Sally sitting side by side on their own little couch:

> *Sally:* Three months later we got married.
> *Harry:* It only took three months.
> *Sally:* Twelve years and three months.
> *Harry:* We had this . . . really wonderful wedding.
> *Sally:* It really was.
> *Harry:* It was great. We had this enormous coconut cake.
> *Sally:* Huge coconut cake with the tiers, and there was this very rich chocolate sauce on the side.
> *Harry:* Right. Because not everyone likes it on the cake, because it makes it very soggy.
> *Sally:* Particularly coconut. It soaks up a lot of that stuff. It's important to keep it on the side.

Harry: Right . . .

And as they continue on, we—

FADE OUT.[121]

This closing scene not only reassures the audience that the couple do indeed end up married—after all the film's obstacles (hindrances real and imagined)—but also emphasizes that these two human beings we've seen bickering, learning, and finding amusement in one another's idiosyncrasies will go on as they have for many years to come. In the interview, they're talking about the dessert that guests ate at their wedding. But what they're really discussing is the long negotiation couples must enter when they sign a marriage contract. How to stack the dishwasher. How to set the thermostat at a temperature that will satisfy no one. How to tolerate or appreciate a partner's strange preferences, the likes and dislikes, that form a personality.

89

Ephron has a gift for addressing the frivolous. Her movies and novels and essays often argue that minor concerns are not trivial. In the title essay of her collection *I Feel Bad About My Neck,* for example, she explores vanity. And where does Ephron's pride reside? It is wrapped in the tubular protrusion of a turtleneck sweater. It lies beneath a silk scarf, under artful folds.

A woman's neck, she explains, reveals its age long before the face begins to wrinkle. "Oh, the neck," sighs Ephron: "There are chicken necks. There are turkey gobbler necks. There are elephant necks. There are necks with wattles and necks with creases on the verge of becoming wattles. There are scrawny necks and fat necks, wrinkled necks, stringy necks, saggy necks, flabby necks, mottled necks."[122]Here's another litany. As with the list-making in Jericho Brown's poem "The Tradition," Ephron uses a catalog to show that the serious can be found in unexpected places. The magic of her incantation—all those distressing, unflattering adjectives, the body made grotesque, flimsy in its aging—is that it reveals the deep fears of the vain. We age. Our faces lose their smoothness, become like craggy rocks on a cliffside.[123]

90

In Peter Shaffer's award-winning play, the character of Antonio Salieri is destabilized by the idea that heavenly compositions could emerge out of someone as frivolous as Wolfgang Amadeus Mozart. Through his vanity, his belief that he should have been made a divine vessel for music, Salieri becomes obsessive, murderous, and suicidal. Hearing one of Mozart's pieces, he is left horrified: "Dimly the music sounded from the salon above. Dimly the stars shone on the street. I was suddenly frightened. It seemed to me I had heard a voice of God—and that it issued from a creature whose own voice I had also heard—and it was the voice of an obscene child!"[124]

Salieri wants to believe that works of genius can be created only by those who are pious and serious. He himself once struck a deal with God. "*Signore,*" he prayed, "let me be a composer! Grant me sufficient fame to enjoy it. In return, I will live in virtue. I will strive to better the lot of my fellows. And I will honor you with music all the days of my life!"[125]

Mozart is neither virtuous nor concerned with improving the lives of others. He is crass. He jokes about farts. His conversations are confettied with childish rhymes and glittering bits of nonsense. He wears gaudy coats and says ridiculous things: "I'm going to pounce-bounce! I'm going to scrunch-munch! I'm going to chew-poo my little mouse-wouse!"[126] Mozart is passionate about his music but also slides too easily between *opera buffa* and *seria*, treating the humorous with the same reverence as he does the dramatic.

Ultimately, Mozart—"spiteful, sniggering, conceited, infantine Mozart"—undoes Salieri's theology.[127] Chosen as a vessel of celestial genius, Mozart becomes a field on which Salieri wages his war against God. Salieri remains the only person in Vienna capable of recognizing the brilliance of *Le nozze di Figaro* and *Don Giovanni*, but he plots Mozart's professional failures, his embarrassments at court, and his reputational disgraces. All this because Mozart is frivolous as a plateful of "Roman chestnuts in brandied sugar" and therefore an unworthy receptacle for musical genius.[128]

91

I once saw a production of *Le nozze di Figaro* at the Santa Fe Opera, the Sangre de Cristo Mountains a glowing pink backdrop to the open-air performance. At the time, my own marriage was a drawing room comedy interrupted by interludes of sadness. Often, I felt as if my husband were disguised as someone else. Or maybe I was the one costumed in this heavy garment called matrimony.

I knew Mozart's opera well, having studied it in college, a year before I met the man who would eventually become my husband. At nineteen, I saw the humor of the piece. But now, well into my thirties, I heard something new in the arias, grief and hurt like the jab of a needle pushed through heavy silk.

Le nozze di Figaro is set over the length of twenty-four hours. It is structured around the classical unities of time, place, and action. Figaro and Susanna, a valet and a maid, prepare for their wedding while their highborn employers, the Count and Countess, struggle with disharmony in their own union. It's an opera about social class, power, and infidelity, how people can remain strangers to one another despite their love.

My favorite moment occurs in the third act. The Countess and Susanna sing a small duet during which they plot with exquisite beauty how to catch the lascivious Count in his infidelity. The Count is determined to have sex with Susanna on her wedding night. He plans to demonstrate his power through the old practice of *droit du seigneur*. This is not medieval France but Seville in the late 1700s. Nonetheless, the Count believes that he has a right to bed Susanna as soon as she has spoken her wedding vows to another man.

So, the Countess dictates a letter to her husband, and Susanna writes, the maid echoing her mistress's words in song. The missive must be in Susanna's script, so that the Count will fall for the ruse and believe she has invited him to make love in the garden, their bodies caressed by summer breezes, touched by the warm tickle of air. The duet is piercing and lovely. As the two sopranos' voices overlap, their notes intertwine like fingers. Briefly held in the charm of their music, the audience forgets that this trick they are playing costs the Countess too much. In the opera's final act, she will dress as Susanna and stand in a shadowed bower until her husband comes to woo her but only because he believes she is someone else. She will feel his misplaced desire—the hurt like a corset pulled too snug against her ribs—as he nudges a glittering ring onto her finger. Eventually, after more disguises and misunderstandings, the couple reconcile in a closing song, all the characters insisting on their sudden contentment.

Despite the lightness of *Le nozze di Figaro,* I've always struggled with the end of the opera: that compulsory joy, the melody tripping over itself in a rush toward resolution. It's hard for me to forget that the Countess must trap her husband. He begs her for forgiveness, *Perdono, perdono,* he pleads, but only after being caught in near-adultery. The Countess must force his love to grow in her direction again, the way a gardener trains a vine with a trellis, the stem of the plant bound or clipped firmly in place. She is often played by some magnificent diva like Kiri Te Kanawa or Renée Fleming, and I hate that a woman with sublime timbre and technique is brought so low that she must trick her spouse back into devotion.

Le nozze di Figaro is classified as opera buffa, a comic opera that features ordinary figures struggling with ordinary problems. Opera buffa is funny, slapstick at times. Certainly, as a genre, it may be called frivolous too. But despite the conventions of the genre, *Le nozze di Figaro* remains tender and affecting.

In *The Impossible Art: Adventures in Opera,* conductor and composer Matthew Aucoin writes about the closing minutes of the opera, when it becomes difficult for the orchestra to keep pace with the singers:

> This moment is challenging for conductors, and the reason has everything to do with the characters' psychological state. . . . The singers inevitably rush here. It's a law of gravity. In no performance *ever* have the singers not felt inclined to push forward at this moment. . . . Even on some rather well-known studio recordings of the opera, singers and orchestra come egregiously unstuck here.
>
> You know what? I think the singers are right. These characters are trying to outrun reality itself. Damn right that they should speed up. It's the conductor's job, and the orchestra's, to keep up with them. The end of *Figaro* should go up in smoke. Heaving examined the heart's every crevice, having exposed every weakness, every selfish or shameful desire, and *still* insisting that love conquers all, there's nothing left to do but light the fireworks.[129]

When the Count asks for forgiveness, Aucoin reads this plea as if it were a supplication. And the Countess, when she responds, has seized control. She forgives him, and "the violins sing a descending arpeggiated figure that . . . is a blessing, light breaking through the clouds."[130] Everyone watching this reconciliation understand that this is "a beautiful illusion."[131] No one's character has been changed by the events of the day. The best that any of us can hope for is "a moment of utter clarity. A sense that it's all beautiful, even if it's not beautiful *for them*. An aerial view of their own souls."

The night that my husband and I watched *Le nozze di Figaro* in Santa Fe, we had been warned to expect a chill, that the temperature would drop after sunset. But it stayed hot long after dark. We sweated in our seats. Sometimes my husband began to drop into sleep, lullabied by the music. His head tilted forward as if he were praying over the paper program in his lap. But as the Count began to beseech, *Perdono, perdono,* I touched my husband's hand to wake him. *Listen,* I whispered, *please, listen—*

92

Listening is never easy. In the classroom, where I teach poetry—how to read it, how to discuss it, how to write it—I sometimes tire of listening. Undeveloped poems can clang or scrape. Sound may be paired with sense nonsensically. Or the poems march across the page, every word too obedient, the meter fascistic and inflexible.

Beyond the music, there may be deeper problems with the text, such as the dexterity of thoughts. Students can lose themselves in a poem's lyricism and forget the story they're telling or what argument they're making. Serious poems are hard to write; they pose intellectual and emotional challenges. To face grief, loss, or trauma and to revise these experiences into art demands an honest assessment of the self. And poems may be unflattering mirrors.[132]

Light verse is even harder to write. As the American poet John Hollander observes,

> "Light verse" need not be pointedly funny, or even (as it tends to be) mildly amusing. Here it should be remembered that, while popular usage suggests that "serious" and "funny" are mutually exclusive opposites, what is funny can also be very serious. This happens most often by design—by the design of wit. Likewise, what is solemn can be deeply frivolous, though usually inadvertently—and

here, again, it will be some kind of wit that points out this shortcoming.[133]

Lightness takes skill. As with almost any craft—the throwing of pots on a wheel, the needling of lacework—light verse needs a delicate, practiced touch. It requires what Hollander calls "a sublimity of surface."[134] He explains that "the one matter about which comic poems often seem avowedly serious is the skill displayed in their own construction."

Hollander was an expert writer of light verse himself. His *Rhyme's Reason: A Guide to English Verse* presents hundreds of fixed forms. But his craft book doesn't read like a dictionary or a dry instruction manual. Instead, his poems are small demonstrations that both define and enact each term's constraints. For example, he writes a villanelle to explain the braided rhymes and maddening refrains of this famous French form. His sonnets show us what this *little song* can do in its Italian and English iterations. His pantoum—a form that came to English poetry via French verse but originated in Malayan tradition—is a witty execution of the poem's recursive lines.

Many students fear rhyme and meter. They dread scansion. Sometimes they believe that formal poetry is the humorless work of dead men from the sixteenth century, stiff poets depicted in oil paintings whose fingers are stained with iron gall ink. But Hollander's poems laugh when laying out the rules of traditional forms. His instructive verse proves it's possible to marry wit to rigorous craft.

I'm also reminded of the American poet and translator Richard Wilbur, who was celebrated for his deft contributions to the lyrics of Leonard Bernstein's operetta *Candide.*

In the song "Glitter and Be Gay," Wilbur pairs "champagne" with "complain" and "lavaliers" with "tears," his rhymes elegant and funny.[135] It's an aria baroque with elaborate trills, difficult runs, a series of notes so high they could shatter a crystal goblet held aloft in the soprano's hand.

In the song, the character of Cunegonde recounts how she has been sold into sexual slavery; her jewels offer comfort now, the pleasure of glitz and scintillation. I once saw a staging of *Candide* in which Cunegonde sang the entire aria from within a clawfoot tub, her costume a flesh-colored leotard covered entirely in plastic, iridescent soap bubbles. The illusion was so convincing that, when Cunegonde suddenly sat upright, the audience gasped, believing for a moment that the singer was naked and soaking wet. And as she belted from the frothy bath, she occasionally lifted a spangled ring or a diamond necklace to catch the light. Wilbur's lyrics sparkled painfully, as Cunegonde alternated between mourning the theft of her innocence and finding joy in the frivolity of glistening things.

Richard Wilbur had a gift for light verse, but he also wrote one of the most poignant poems about being a poet that I know. In the "The Writer," a speaker overhears his daughter typing in her room upstairs. At first, he is dismissive of her efforts, glibly wishing her "a lucky passage."[136] As if responding to this flippant thought, the whole house seems to quiet, and the speaker recalls a bird trapped in that same upstairs room a few years before. It takes five, painful stanzas for the bird to wing its way free. The speaker remembers how the "iridescent creature" knocked "against the brilliance" of a closed window, falling to the ground, falling as it tried to get out. But, at last, after many attempts, the bird managed to escape, "clearing the sill of the world." The poem closes with the speaker regretting his earlier lack of respect for his daughter's efforts. He comes to recognize that, like the trapped starling, all writers—both the young and the experienced—may fail to find words that soar. But it's our effort to crash "against the brilliance" of language that matters.

Although "The Writer" couldn't be more different from "Glitter and Be Gay," the two texts share a commitment to poetic craft. They're both equally serious about syntax, the handling of narrative, the lyric power of the line. Students frequently write light verse because they wish to avoid speaking in a vulnerable voice. They worry that earnestness is *cringe*. They think frivolity will allow them to circumvent the frightening parts of being alive. But they lack training and craft; without poetic technique, light verse becomes little more than a punch line broken into stanzas, a knock-knock joke.

Of course, as Hollander asserts, light verse can be very serious. Take Dorothy Parker's "Résumé," a poem in which a wry speaker presents a catalog of ways to off herself.[137] She runs through her options, identifying the problem with each method of dying. Parker uses short and incisive lines, cutting rhymes, as if to demonstrate how language itself can nick. Scalpel-like, the speaker slashes through each option. Razors? No. Drowning. Nope. Acid or pills? Nah. A bullet? A rope? An oven, a car's exhaust? Scratch each one off the list. Every method has its drawback. Some are uncomfortable, others disfiguring. Death, the speaker implies, should not inconvenience us or break the law. In the end, she argues that we "might as well" choose life, not because there's anything valuable in survival but because the alternatives are all so rotten.

The poem's river predicts Virginia Woolf in 1941, as she loaded the pockets of her coat with stones. The gas anticipates Sylvia Plath, who killed herself in 1963. Death: by carbon monoxide poisoning, that infamous oven puffing out its poison. "Résumé" foresees Anne Sexton's suicide too. But this verse isn't meant to be a prophecy about the deaths of poets. It's simply a list composed by a speaker who has thought carefully about the possibility of her own suicide, a grim recitation of the many ways she has imagined killing herself.

"Resumé" illustrates Hollander's contention that "metrical perfection and even ingenuity" are "necessary in order for comic verse to be acutely witty."[138] There is nothing unserious about Parker's frivolity. The poem is indeed acute. That is, it ends with a sharpened point.

93

In *On Tyranny,* Timothy Snyder provides readers with a different kind of list, advising us on steps we might take to resist the rise of autocracy. Snyder's lessons are derived from his training as a historian of twentieth century Central and Eastern European history. Although his is a book filled with warnings about the skulking threat of despotism—including chapters with titles like "Do Not Obey in Advance," "Defend Institutions," and "Believe in Truth"—his twelfth piece of advice might surprise. "Make Eye contact and Small Talk," Snyder recommends:

> This is not just polite. It is part of being a citizen and a responsible member of society. It is also a way to stay in touch with your surroundings, break down social barriers, and understand whom you should and should not trust. If we enter a culture of denunciation, you will want to know the psychological landscape of your daily life.[139]

As the daughter of two American Foreign Service officers, every day I observed the importance of small talk to my parents' work overseas. When we lived in communist Poland in the 1980s, my mother and father often relied on pleasantries and chitchat to develop their professional contacts. Polite conversation could lead to information, a valuable form of capital in diplomatic circles.

Warsaw always seemed ash gray in those years, the sky darkening to charcoal in the winter months. The city wasn't considered as dangerous as Moscow, but the State Department designated it a *hardship post.*

Every few months, we drove to West Berlin. The U.S. embassy in Warsaw had a small, low-ceilinged commissary on the first floor of one of the buildings, a place to buy coffee or a box of cereal in its narrow aisles. But most of the American employees made regular expeditions to Germany to stock up on food, household goods, toiletries, and other supplies that were impossible to find in Poland. On any day in Warsaw, there were lines around the block for whatever item a shop was suddenly selling. This could mean loaves of seedless ryebread, dull rolls of toilet paper, the occasional tin of chicory coffee. It wasn't uncommon for people to stand in a queue without knowing what they were waiting to buy. There was, of course, a black market for everything. Frivolities were particularly dear: chocolate, bootlegged cassette tapes, flacons of French perfume. Things could also be purchased with bribes; a bottle of vodka or a carton of cigarettes might be traded for a place setting of hand-painted porcelain or perhaps a hunk of amber washed up on the sandy shores of Gdańsk.

In my memories, the trip to West Berlin took several long days across pitted roads. We always spent the night in Poznań, the midpoint between the two cities, where there was a U.S. consulate. In the morning, we would return to the route again. As I recall it, by early or late afternoon, we were parked at Checkpoint Charlie, waiting to cross over into West Berlin. My father rolled down the window, handing our three passports to the East German guard who eyed the dark blue covers warily: American diplomats. Then the man would sigh and walk away, our documents held tightly in his gloved hands.

We might sit there then for an hour, the car in park, exhaust puffing into the cold air like nervous breaths. My parents didn't need to tell me, *Behave*. Waiting at the border, I found it easy to read menace in the scene. I knew I must sit motionless in the back seat, my mouth a pink line of silence. Through the window, I watched the men in their woolen uniforms. Often, they wore some kind of long weapon slung on a strap over their shoulders. Perhaps, one guard was on a phone. Or another was holding up paperwork that needed official stamps. And though we seldom waited longer than sixty minutes, my parents often seemed anxious. My father fidgeted with the dials on the radio. My mother ate the last few bites of a cheese sandwich she had prepared that morning, flicking crumbs from her lap. Occasionally, there was small talk in the car as well. My parents—both of them the children of Jewish refugees, both raised in German-speaking households—would roll down a window, calling out courteously to a guard, *Entschuldigung!*

When I look now at a map, I realize that the distance between Warsaw and West Berlin is less than six hundred kilometers. Today, it's a trip that wouldn't take more than six hours. And although the roads were probably bumpier and less well marked in the 1980s than they are now, I can't imagine that the journey took significantly longer back then. In other words, the distance I remember is not one of geography but rather it was the feeling of driving from deprivation into frivolous plenty, into a city of strudel and infinite cups of hot cocoa, which is to say, it was like traveling from one world into another.

94

And on the morning after a presidential election—worried and scared about the future—I stood in my closet, organizing what I would wear for the next week. These jeans with this blouse and a red belt at my waist. This camel blazer paired with black slacks. This suede jacket. This scarf sad as a field of autumn flowers.

I stood in my bathroom and swiped a layer of mineralized mud across my face until I seemed hidden behind a green-gray mask. I let it harden on my skin. Then I washed it away.

I polished my jewelry, rubbed at the tarnish with a soft cloth. The action was in my control: to bring a shine to these small spots of darkness.

A friend texted me, saying, *I made biscuits because I needed to make something. Really hard to keep moving though that's all there is to do.*

A few minutes later, I stood in the kitchen and watched my coffee drip into a ceramic mug glazed the color of wet earth. My father—who used to be a professor of classical French literature—quoted the final line of Voltaire's *Candide*. He was standing there in his bathrobe; the blue flannel slumped over his shoulders in worn, defeated folds. "Il faut cultiver notre Jardin," he shrugged.[140] We must cultivate our garden.

For Voltaire, abstract philosophies will not do. He believes in building little places of safety. We must encourage delicate plants to bloom. We must create our own prelapsarian landscapes, although our gardens may be narrow and bounded by flimsy wooden fences. Nothing is coming to rescue us—not the divine and certainly not optimistic maxims about the goodness of the world.

In an essay about *Candide*, Adam Gopnik explains,

> the force of that last great injunction, "We must cultivate our garden," is that our responsibility is local, and concentrated on immediate action. . . . The horror that Voltaire wanted crushed, cruelty in the name of God and civilization, was a specific and contingent thing. His satire of optimism is in this sense an optimistic book—optimistic not only in its gaiety, which implies the possibility of seeing things as they are, but also in its argument. Voltaire did not believe that there was any justice or balance in the world, but he believed that bad ideas made people bad. . . . He knew that the flood would get your garden no matter what

> you did; but you could at least try to keep the priests and the policemen off the grass. It wasn't enough, but it was something.[141]

My father and I looked through the sliding glass doors and out at the backyard, where the beginnings of a new garden were beginning to grow. Just a few days before, my husband had planted a pair of desert willows on each side of a slab of local stone. They leaned toward each other, their branches bending over the rock, as if engaged in a private conversation. It would be months—maybe longer than that—before the two trees offered up their first flowers, floppy purple blossoms smelling slightly of sugar. It might be years before the garden was established, each shrub and bush able to resist the hard rains and the unexpected sun, every stem stable, deeply rooted in the soil.

95

And many months from now, there are marches in the streets, national demonstrations against tyranny. People come dressed as gray sharks and carry signs that read: *DON'T TAKE THEIR BAIT!* They are costumed as Coney Island hotdogs, purple monsters, the Statue of Liberty. "This humorous form of protest, known as tactical frivolity, shows the absurdity of the charge that all the protesters are armed militants," novelist Gary Shteyngart explains in an essay about the phenomenon. "It's hard to call an inflatable chicken dangerous."[142]

Tactical frivolity has its roots in ancient Greek theater where comedy and myth are used to critique the Athenian state. *Brekekekeks koaks koaks,* says a chorus of frogs, mocking Dionysus. Tactical frivolity is connected to carnivals and clowns, as well as to François Rabelais's Gargantua and Pantagruel, how the writer merges the satirical with the philosophical.

Melissa W. Wilcox, a scholar of religious studies, calls this kind of activism "serious parody." In her book *Queer Nuns,* she discusses the Sisters of Perpetual Indulgence, a multinational order of queer and trans activists whose mission includes doing charitable works, creating performance pieces, and engaging in efforts to reform the Catholic Church. As Wilcox understands it, serious parody "simultaneously critiques and reclaims cultural traditions in the interest of supporting the lives and political objectives of marginalized groups."[143] She argues that the Sisters represent "a form of cultural protest in which a disempowered group parodies an oppressive cultural institution while simultaneously claiming for itself what it believes to be an equally good or superior enactment of one or more culturally respected aspects of that same institution."[144] Serious parody is compelling because the outsiders are also insiders. While the Sisters of Perpetual Indulgence is not an order recognized by the Vatican, their criticisms emerge from a commitment to—rather than a rejection of—Roman Catholicism.

As with serious parody, tactical frivolity is intentional foolishness. The trivial is deployed deliberately. Humor disarms power with cheeky placards and silly outfits. "Once the pants are lowered and the undies of the despot are glimpsed," Shteyngart explains, "there is no point of return."[145] The ruler who wishes to handcuff dissent struggles with political speech as whoopie cushion, protest as pie in the face. The jester, after all, is often the only figure in court able to poke fun at the monarch. He stays safe, thanks to his foolscap that jingles with bells and to the small scepter he carries, called a marotte, a bauble topped with a grinning face.

Shteyngart—a Russian Jew whose family emigrated from the Soviet Union in 1979 to escape persecution—understands the ways that comedy can be used to subvert the autocrat. His own fiction frequently engages in tactical frivolity for the sake of social critique. In an interview about what it means to be a Soviet Jew, Shteyngart says: "We lived in a totalitarian system for 70 years where a lot was lost. Jewish humor interests me the most, and Soviet Jewish humor is Jewish humor taken to the max. It's Jewish humor from the edge of the grave."[146]

The protesters too stand at the edge of a grave. They are hoping the frivolous can save us.

96

And many months ago, I was on an airplane. From behind the anonymity of my paper face mask, I watched a teenage girl. I could see her between the gap of the two seats in front of me. She kept turning her phone into a mirror. It must have been an app, the edges of the reflection made to appear eroded, like a piece of glass where the silver backing has begun to flake off.

For twenty minutes, she held the mirror at different angles and distances from her skin. Far away to take in the entire visage. Close up to exam the curve of her nostrils, how gaping the pores. She was young and while, perhaps, mostly beautiful thanks to her winged eyeliner and peach lip gloss, I felt sorry for how deeply she was captured by her own image. I wondered who had made her think that the minutest details of her face should matter so much.

Someone watching me in the Year of Perfect Skin could have asked these same questions about my gestures.

Katherine Indermaur writes about facial and body dysmorphia in her book-length lyric essay *I|I*. For her, the mirror prompts philosophical meditations and poetic visions as much as it remains a source of self-castigation:

> In a yoga class, I|I heard a woman confess that she thought her pregnancies would cure her of anorexia. They didn't, granting instead a deeper nuance to her dysmorphia, knowing her body was capable of growing then birthing then nursing and still seeing wrong, seeing fat.
>
> I|I confess that I|I, too, have held this hope—that being pregnant might purify me|me of my|my desire to cause my|self harm, that seeing my|self as a vessel for another would keep me|me from hurting my|my child, thus from hurting my|self.[147]

The lyric essay may function like a hall of mirrors, reflections reflecting reflections. The text provides no escape from disorder. Instead, both reader and writer are trapped within a glittering infinity of echoing surfaces. The mirror's glimmer is seductive. So too the sheen of lyricism.

That's the trap of this book as well. In writing lyrically about the frivolous, might my prose—and the anxiety that sits behind my words—fall into frivolity?[148]

We hate Narcissus for tumbling into his own watery reflection. His myth gives us narcissism, a personality disorder without cure. But maybe we should empathize with this kind of drowning regard for the self. Narcissus is a flower. Narcissus is a compulsion. A face that can't stop staring at itself is really searching for a way to fall asleep or melt into numbness.

Perhaps, the longer the girl on the airplane stared at herself the drowsier she became, tranquilized and unable to wake, while the world continued to clang around her.

97

Not long before his death, writer Italo Calvino prepared a series of lectures that he was supposed to give at Harvard University. The first of these focuses on the quality of lightness in literature, which he characterizes as a virtue. To explain lightness, Calvino cites the myth of Perseus, the Greek hero who once slayed a snake-haired woman, her image so terrifying that she could turn others to granite with her gaze. "From Medusa's blood a winged horse, Pegasus, is born; the heaviness of stone is transformed into its opposite, and with the stamp of a single hoof on Mount Helicon, a fountain springs forth from which the Muses drink."[149] A writer's handling of lightness and weight are contrasting approaches, just as Pegasus—a great horse who gallops on the breezes—is an antonym to Medusa.

Later, after speaking about Ovid and Lucretius, for both of whom "lightness is a way of seeing the world" as well as "something created in the writing," Calvino goes on to consider Boccaccio's *Decameron* and Dante's *Divine Comedy*.[150] He observes that lightness and weight "have competed over the centuries" in European literature: "one that seeks to make language a weightless element that hovers over things like a cloud, or, better, a fine dust, or, better still, a magnetic field; another that seeks to imbue language with the weight and thickness and concreteness of objects and bodies and sensations."[151] Then, Calvino addresses Shakespeare's Puck—that merry and wandering sprite whose every word is fairy-winged—and Hamlet, whose voice blends "melancholy and humor."[152] Calvino gives us Cyrano de Bergerac too. And he closes with Kafka, examining a short story in which a coal bucket lifts fantastically into the air before it "disappears beyond the Ice Mountains."[153] In each example Calvino provides, the writing contains images of lightness or engages in a philosophical study of light things; most importantly, the narrator speaks lightly in a voice that glints with slyness.

Throughout the lecture, Calvino's primary concern is for what writing will become in the twenty-first century. He hopes that it will be defined by lightness. "That is how we, astride our bucket, will face the new millennium," he says, "without hoping to find there anything more than we're able to bring with us."[154] In other words, Calvino imagines a literature that packs light, that is fleet-footed, that ascends.

I'm not sure what Calvino would have made of the Year of Perfect Skin or of my efforts to record that era, which was also the period of our global pandemic. Writing a defense of frivolity demands a prose that is both light and weighty. Pegasus and Medusa. The one creature leaps, and his feathers catch the current, lifting him easily, up, up, into the thin air of ideas. The other creature is a monster; trauma has made her face unbearable to others, Medusa raped by the sea-god who pinned her to the ground in

Athena's temple, while the girl twisted beneath his muscled bulk. No one came to save her. Now her weeping turns men to stone.

98

Whenever I complain about aging, my mother tells me, "Well, it beats the alternative." She means death, I suppose.

Skin is the body's largest organ. We cannot survive without it. To be flayed is excruciating and deadly torture. In 135 CE, Rabbi Akiva was murdered by the Romans for teaching the Torah, his body flayed with iron combs and his final words the Sh'ma, the most essential of all Jewish prayers. Saints are often flayed, traitors too, as well as generals on the losing sides of wars and leaders of failed uprisings. A body flayed has been stripped of its protection. Without skin, we are more than naked; we are shamefully opened.

Often in the weeks before death, a person's skin thins. It blotches or speckles. It pales into grayness. Hands and feet mottle.

99

In the Year of Perfect Skin, my immersion in the mirror became a way of watching for the first signs of my diminishment, my disappearance, my death.

Frivolity itself is an effort to perfect what appears to be merely skin deep. It celebrates what floats on the surface of things. Some frivolities require craftsmanship, an artisan's certain hands. Some provide necessary diversions, particularly in dark times when the streets beyond our windows are suddenly shadowed with threats of illness or autocracy, the return of ancient hatreds. The frivolous may summon us back to ourselves. Frivolity calls us to our bodies, which crave pleasure and joy, a dusty sweetness on the tip of the tongue.

100

Some frivolities wear satin bows or ribbons to conceal their solemnity. Some frivolous things stand close to the serious, the two not that far apart but existing on a continuum. In fact, it feels increasingly tired to pit frivolity against the serious. Nearly every discussion of a frivolous pursuit seems to begin with this binary, as when dance critic Alastair Macaulay is forced to ask,

> Is ballet a serious art or a frivolous one? Very often, it's both at the same time. Since frivolous means "lacking in seriousness"—also lightweight, flippant, of little weight or importance—that would seem a contradiction in terms.
>
> But ballet abounds in self-contradictions. It continually shows mere mortals becoming works of ideal geometry, and helps us see music in terms of three-dimensional space. It can turn silliness into enchantment, make myth real, or—even in a work of pure dance—make us feel how the sublime coexists with the comic. With equal ease, alas, it can turn musical masterworks into dance cliché or literary classics into fatuous jollifications.[155]

Macaulay knows there's nothing unserious about an art form that requires such discipline, talent, or pain. Ballet's geometric precision demands impossible flexibility. It requires a kind of strength that makes every movement appear unforced and natural, as if a body were meant to tilt back into open space, held aloft by a single hand.

Decades ago, when I was a child in Warsaw, a renowned prima ballerina came to dinner at my parents' house. Earlier that day, I had seen her dance and had marveled at the perfect curve of a foot perched en pointe, every finger-flit effortless as a butterfly's wings, each leap as if she were returning her body to its rightful place in the high air. From far away, she looked like a black crinoline skirt balanced on a pair of reeds, slender stems that moved with the breezes. It was only when she sat in our living room that I noticed the corded muscles in her arms and neck. Her feet—no longer satin-bound but resting in a pair of flats—were fixed in a permanent arch. The bones clenched. The skin was rubbed red from practicing at the barre. Is ballet frivolous? Her body's visible hurt gave me an answer. *No.*

Even frivolity for the sake of frivolity may have value in that it entertains. But, always, the frivolous asks us to examine what we find worthy and what we dismiss. And what prejudices push us to make such distinctions?

101

In the Year of Perfect Skin, I learned that skin is perpetually imperfectible. Caring for it may be frivolous. Still, skin deserves kindness because, in the end, it is not like a piece of rare pottery to be displayed behind plexiglass. It is lived in. It is roughhoused. It is pinched or stitched. It is waxed. Depilated. It is shaved or tweezed or plucked. It is poked with a needle. It absorbs all brutalities of weather and sun. It bends to our expressions. It wrinkles with feeling. It suffers our judgments. It is stretched and squeezed and studied beneath bright lights, a curving glass that magnifies each flaw. It is nicked and scraped. It is sandpapered smooth. It is washed into redness. It tries to retain elasticity and bounce. It ages. It shows time on its surface. And, more than anything, skin—this gooseflesh, this covering, this thick or thin—skin does its best to endure.[156]

Acknowledgments

Several excerpts from *Frivolity* appeared previously in my "Sillage" perfume column for *Aromatica Poetica*.

Many thanks to Costica Bradatan and Wendy Lochner for their encouragement and support throughout the process of writing this book.

Thank you also to Annette Becker of the Texas Fashion Collection at the University of North Texas, Dacy Gillespie, Timothy Schaffert, and Victor Wong for being so generous with your time and knowledge.

A special thanks to my parents. Even when you haven't always understood why I love these things, you have celebrated my passion for frippery and folly.

And to my husband, Jeremy—thank you for joining me on so many silly excursions. Frivolity is loveliest when it's shared with you.

Notes

1. Reader, would you like a few synonyms? How about *folly, frippery, fun.* Also *flightiness, flirting, fribble.*
2. We might think of it as another F-word. Frivolity is taboo. It should elicit fear and shame, like cannibalism or incest, like politics at the dinner table, like asking a colleague about their paycheck, like picking one's nose in public.
3. Frivolity is a provocation. And shame on me for wanting to be a thing of shimmer and seduction.
4. John Berger, *Ways of Seeing* (1972; Penguin, 1990), 51.
5. George Eliot, *Middlemarch* (1871–72; Penguin Classics, 2003), 8.
6. Eliot, *Middlemarch*, 9.
7. Pamela Erens, "It Can Be Embarrassing to Love Dorothea," *Paris Review*, August 8, 2013, https://www.theparisreview.org/blog/2013/08/08/it-can-be-embarrassing-to-love-dorothea/.
8. Michel Montaigne, "Of Vanity," *The Complete Essays of Montaigne*, trans. Donald M. Frame (Stanford University Press, 1965), 721.
9. Montaigne, "Of Vanity," *Complete Essays*, 766.
10. Victor Brombert, "Lessons of Montaigne," *The Pensive Citadel* (University of Chicago Press, 2023), 90.
11. Montaigne, "We Taste Nothing Pure," *Complete Essays*, 510.
12. Sianne Ngai, *Our Aesthetic Categories: Zany, Cute, Interesting* (Harvard University Press, 2015), 1.

13. Ngai, *Our Aesthetic*, 7.
14. Ngai, *Our Aesthetic*, 3.
15. Ngai, *Our Aesthetic*, 5.
16. Susan Sontag, "Notes on Camp," *Against Interpretation: And Other Essays* (Picador, 1961), 275.
17. Sontag, "Notes on Camp," *Against*, 283.
18. Sontag, "Notes on Camp," *Against*, 276.
19. Sei Shōnagon, *The Pillow Book*, trans. Meredith McKinney (Penguin Classics, 2007), xxviii.
20. Shōnagon, *Pillow Book*, ix.
21. Shōnagon, *Pillow Book*, 148.
22. Shōnagon, *Pillow Book*, 87.
23. Shōnagon, *Pillow Book*, 88.
24. Or what of the delicate frivolities of Sei Shōnagon? When she speaks of a skein of wild geese in the autumn sky, I too watch the birds from a hillside. I can see the shape their bodies form, like a necklace strung across the shadowed neck of night.
25. Arika Okrent, "The Listicle as a Literary Form," *University of Chicago Magazine*, January–February 2014, https://mag.uchicago.edu/arts-humanities/listicle-literary-form.
26. Jericho Brown, "The Tradition," *The Tradition* (Copper Canyon Press, 2019), 10.
27. George Orwell, *1984* (1949; Signet Classic, 1961), 283.
28. William Strunk Jr. and E. B. White, *The Elements of Style*, 4th ed. (Allyn & Bacon, 2000), 34.
29. Maybe scholarship needs this kind of fervor too. Couldn't there be space—if we are brave enough—not only for the methodical footsteps of critical thinking but also for the speckled mark? Couldn't we make room for the downward line that ends in a brief, ecstatic dot? Couldn't we? Couldn't! We!
30. Stephen Spector, *The Quotable Guide to Punctuation* (Oxford University Press, 2017), 183.
31. Emma Goldberg, "Where Do We Stand on the Exclamation Point?," *New York Times*, September 27, 2019, https://www.nytimes.com/2019/09/27/style/exclamation-points.html.
32. Gertrude Stein, *Lectures in America* (Beacon Press, 1935), 214.
33. Stein, *Lectures*, 215.

34. Emily Dickinson, *The Poems of Emily Dickinson*, ed. R. W. Franklin (Belknap Press, 1998), 87.
35. Dickinson, *Poems*, 11.
36. Or I can wander, in the playfulness of my imagination, through Dickinson's green and tangled gardens. Reader, let's to go to her room wallpapered in pink roses. We can sit at her desk. We can touch the poems bundled into a form she called fascicles.
37. John T. Frederick, "Hawthorne's 'Scribbling Women,'" *New England Quarterly*, June 1975, https://www.jstor.org/stable/364660?seq=1.
38. Arthur C. Danto, *What Art Is* (Yale University Press, 2014), 44.
39. Danto, *Art*, 45.
40. Is vanity another reason to feel ashamed?
41. Jacob Grimm and Wilhem Grimm, *The Original Folk and Fairy Tales of the Brothers Grimm: The Complete First Edition*, trans. Jack Zipes (Princeton University Press, 2014), 170.
42. Grimm, *Original Folk*, 178.
43. We never see little Snow White age past her beauty. The story ends on her wedding day. But thirty years later? Perhaps, she might resemble her mother, not only physically but in her fury at what has been stolen from her face each day. On her fiftieth birthday, little Snow White might slam her fist against the mirror and break the glass.
44. Anna Broadway, "Pink Wasn't Always Girly," *Atlantic*, August 12, 2013, www.theatlantic.com/sexes/archive/2013/08/pink-wasnt-always-girly/278535/.
45. David Batchelor, *Chromophobia* (Reaktion Books, 2000), 22.
46. Batchelor, *Chromophobia*, 22–23.
47. Kassia St. Claire, *The Secret Lives of Color* (Penguin Books, 2017), 29.
48. St. Claire, *Secret Lives*, 116.
49. Jake Newsome, *Pink Triangle Legacies: Coming Out in the Shadow of the Holocaust* (Cornell University Press, 2022), 15.
50. Maria Teresa Hart, *Doll* (Bloomsbury Academic, 2022), 15.
51. Hart, *Doll*, 35.
52. Vanessa Friedman, "All Pinked Out," *New York Times*, July 24, 2023, www.nytimes.com/2023/07/24/style/all-pinked-out.html.
53. Helen O'Hara, "The Best Thing About the Barbie Movie? It's Going to Annoy All the Right People," *Stylist*, July 21, 2023, www.stylist.co.uk/entertainment/film/barbie-movie-feminist-backlash/805957.

54. Chavisa Woods, "The Insidious Faux-Feminism of Barbie," *Full Stop*, August 7, 2023, www.full-stop.net/2023/08/07/features/essays/chavisa-woods/the-insidious-faux-feminism-of-barbie/?utm_source=substack&utm_medium=email.
55. Carol Hay, "Barbie Used to Be Everything Wrong with Patriarchal Beauty Ideals, Feminist Professor Says. Now She's Closer to 'Queer Camp,'" *Fortune* magazine, July 17, 2023, https://fortune.com/2023/07/17/barbie-movie-beauty-standards-patriarchy-queer-camp-femmephobia-feminism-scholar.
56. Juan Barquin, "On Barbie and Greta Gerwig's Colorful, Complicated Portrait of Humanity," *Autostraddle*, July 21, 2023, https://www.autostraddle.com/barbie-review.
57. Timothy Schaffert, interview by Jehanne Dubrow, video conference, August 9, 2024.
58. Michèle Roberts, preface to *Madame Bovary* by Gustave Flaubert (Penguin Classics, 1992), vii.
59. Flaubert, *Bovary*, 76.
60. Flaubert, *Bovary*, 115–116.
61. The first time I read *Madame Bovary*, it seemed that Flaubert was reprimanding me. Didn't I share Emma's love of shopping? Didn't I exhibit all the worst traits of the petite bourgeoisie? Didn't I deserve her poisonous, painful ending?
62. Jane Austen, *Pride and Prejudice*, vol. 2 of *The Oxford Illustrated Jane Austen* (Oxford University Press, 1988), 348.
63. Janes Austen, *"Northanger Abbey" and "Persuasion,"* vol. 5 of *The Oxford Illustrated Jane Austen* (Oxford University Press, 1988), 73.
64. Janes Austen, *Emma*, vol. 4 of *The Oxford Illustrated Jane Austen* (Oxford University Press, 1988), 484.
65. Austen, *Emma*, 433.
66. Austen, *Pride*, 36.
67. Austen, *Pride*, 310.
68. Austen, *Pride*, 310–11.
69. Thorstein Veblen, *The Theory of the Leisure Class* (1899; Oxford University Press, 2007), 7.
70. Veblen, *Leisure Class*, 113.
71. Veblen, *Leisure Class*, 113.
72. Veblen, *Leisure Class*, 120.

73. What do I hate about my hips? Why do I worry about the soft skin on my upper arms? Which inches on my body cause me the most embarrassment?
74. Dacy Gillespie, interview by Jehanne Dubrow, video conference, August 30, 2024.
75. Rebecca Arnold, *Fashion: A Very Short Introduction* (Oxford University Press, 2009), 4.
76. Arnold, *Fashion*, 7.
77. Jonah Weiner, "Why Are Pants So Big (Again)?," *New York Times*, March 3, 2024, https://www.nytimes.com/2024/03/03/magazine/big-pants-style.html.
78. Barbara Carnevali, *Social Appearances: A Philosophy of Display and Prestige*, trans. Zakiya Hanafi (Columbia University Press, 2020), 6–7.
79. Carnevali, *Appearances*, 23.
80. Annette Becker, interview by Jehanne Dubrow, Texas Fashion Collection, University of North Texas, June 22, 2022.
81. Evening ensemble, Texas Fashion Collection, University of North Texas, https://digital.library.unt.edu/ark:/67531/metadc955546/?q=future%20of%20fashion.
82. Doesn't frivolity contain many of these same contrasts—the hard and the soft, the glass bead and the downy feather?
83. Stephanie L. Herdrich, "Madame X," *Fashioned by Sargent*, ed. Erica E. Hirshler et al. (MFA Publications, 2023), 36.
84. Herdrich, "X," *Fashioned*, 39.
85. D. H Lawrence, *D. H. Lawrence: Late Essays and Articles*, ed. James T. Boulton (Cambridge University Press, 2014), 194.
86. Chris Wiley, "When Lee Miller Took a Bath in Hitler's Tub," *New Yorker*, January 9, 2024, https://www.newyorker.com/culture/photo-booth/when-lee-miller-took-a-bath-in-hitlers-tub.
87. Victor Wong, interview by Jehanne Dubrow, email, September 7, 2024.
88. Jehanne Dubrow, "Rabbit," package insert for Zoologist Perfumes.
89. Richard Adams, *Watership Down* (1972; Scribner, 2005), 29.
90. Madeline Miller, introduction to *Watership*, xiii.
91. Jehanne Dubrow, *throughsmoke: an essay in notes* (New Rivers Press, 2019), 1.
92. Dubrow, *throughsmoke*, 84.

93. Perfume remains a pleasure for which I feel compelled to apologize. But why such guilt in seeking out a small bottle of indulgence? Where is the shame in loving an aromatic likeness of the soul?
94. Yasmina Reza, "The Fabric of Life: An Interview with Yasmina Reza," interview by Violane Huisman, *Paris Review*, February 20, 2015, www.theparisreview.org/blog/2015/02/20/the-fabric-of-a-life-an-interview-with-yasmina-reza.
95. Yasmina Reza, *God of Carnage*, trans. Christophere Hampton (Farrar, Straus and Giroux, 2008), 18.
96. Reza, *Carnage*, 27.
97. Henrik Ibsen, *A Doll's House and Other Plays*, trans. Deborah Dawkin and Erik Skuggevik (Penguin Classics, 2016), 110.
98. Ibsen, *Doll's House*, 113.
99. Ibsen, *Doll's House*, 182.
100. Katherine May, *Wintering: The Power of Rest and Retreat in Difficult Times* (Riverhead Books, 2020), 14.

101. Jia Tolentino, "The Year that Skin Care Became a Coping Mechanism," *New Yorker*, December 18, 2017, www.newyorker.com/culture/cultural-comment/the-year-that-skin-care-became-a-coping-mechanism.
102. Blaise Pascal, *Pensées*, trans. A. J. Krailsheimer (Penguin Classics, 1995), 38.
103. Pascal, *Pensées*, 68.
104. Montaigne, "Of Vanity," *Complete Essays*, 766.
105. Pascal, *Pensées*, 67.
106. Pascal, *Pensées*, 95.
107. Pascal, *Pensées*, 57.
108. Hello, reader. Are you still following me through the ornament and organza?
109. Griselda Pollock, "The Overlooked Radicalism of Impressionist Mary Cassatt," *Frieze*, September 3, 2018, www.frieze.com/article/overlooked-radicalism-impressionist-mary-cassatt.
110. Mark Doty, *Dog Years* (HarperCollins, 2007), 2.
111. Doty, *Dog*, 2–3.
112. Doty, *Dog*, 4.
113. William Shakespeare, *A Midsummer Night's Dream*, in *The Oxford Shakespeare: The Complete Works*, 2nd ed., ed. Stanley Wells, Gary Taylor,

John Jowett, and William Montgomery (Oxford University Press, 2005), 1.1.134.

114. Shakespeare, *A Midsummer Night's Dream*, 3.2.117.
115. Stanley Cavell, *Pursuits of Happiness: The Hollywood Comedy of Remarriage* (Harvard University Press, 1981), 1.
116. Cavell, *Pursuits*, 8.
117. Cavell, *Pursuits*, 15.
118. Cavell, *Pursuits*, 7.
119. Caryn James, "It's Harry [Loves] Sally in a Romance of New Yorkers and Neuroses," *New York Times*, July 12, 1989, www.nytimes.com/1989/07/12/movies/review-film-it-s-harry-loves-sally-in-a-romance-of-new-yorkers-and-neuroses.html.
120. Nora Ephron, *When Harry Met Sally* (Knopf, 1990), xi.
121. Ephron, *Harry*, 98.
122. Nora Ephron, *I Feel Bad About My Neck* (Knopf, 2006), 5.
123. My own vanity exists in a tiled room bright with shame. There's terror too, but why? I am afraid of my skin's imperfections. Afraid of becoming increasingly less appealing, not only to others but also to myself. Afraid that, one day, I will be alone and anonymous.
124. Peter Shaffer, *Amadeus* (1979; Harper Perennial, 2001), 28.
125. Shaffer, *Amadeus*, 17.
126. Shaffer, *Amadeus*, 25.
127. Shaffer, *Amadeus*, 59.
128. Shaffer, *Amadeus*, 53.
129. Matthew Aucoin, *The Impossible Art: Adventures in Opera* (Farrar, Straus and Giroux, 2021), 286.
130. Aucoin, *Impossible*, 284.
131. Aucoin, *Impossible*, 285.
132. Is this essay an unflattering mirror as well? Reader, do you hate what you see in these ugly words?
133. John Hollander, ed., *American Wits: An Anthology of Light Verse* (Library of America, 2003), xviii.
134. Hollander, *Wits*, xix.
135. Richard Wilbur, "Glitter and Be Gay," *Collected Poems: 1943–2004* (Ecco, 2006), 468–69.
136. Wilbur, "The Writer," *Collected*, 128.

137. Dorothy Parker, "Résumé," in *American Wits: An Anthology of Light Verse*, ed. John Hollander (Library of America, 2003), 86.
138. Hollander, *Wits*, xix.
139. Timothy Snyder, *On Tyranny: Twenty Lessons from the Twentieth Century* (Crown, 2017), 81.
140. Voltaire, *Candide ou l'optimisme* (Gallimard, 2003), 130.
141. Adam Gopnik, "Voltaire's Garden," *New Yorker*, February 27, 2005, https://www.newyorker.com/magazine/2005/03/07/voltaires-garden.
142. Gary Shteyngart, "The Rise of the Inflatable Chicken Resistance," *New York Times*, October 20, 2025, https://www.nytimes.com/2025/10/20/opinion/no-kings-protest-chicago-tactical-frivolity.html.
143. Melissa W. Wilcox, *Queer Nuns: Religion, Activism, and Serious Parody* (New York University Press, 2018), 2.
144. Wilcox, *Nuns*, 70.
145. Gary Shteyngart, "Inflatable Chicken," https://www.nytimes.com/2025/10/20/opinion/no-kings-protest-chicago-tactical-frivolity.html.
146. Gary Shteyngart, "Q&A with Russian Jewish Writer Gary Shteyngart," interview by Harry Wiland, *Jewish Journal*, September 7, 2006, https://jewishjournal.com/culture/arts/13641/.
147. Katherine Indermaur, *I/I* (Seneca Review Books, 2022), 53.
148. Tell me: What is the line between defending the frivolous and becoming it?
149. Italo Calvino, *Six Memos for the Next Millennium*, trans. Geoffrey Brock (Mariner Classics, 2016), 5.
150. Calvino, *Memos*, 11.
151. Calvino, *Memos*, 18.
152. Calvino, *Memos*, 23.
153. Calvino, *Memos*, 34.
154. Calvino, *Memos*, 35.
155. Alastair Macaulay, "On the Frivolities of Ballet, the Contradictory Art," *New York Times*, May 19, 2017, www.nytimes.com/2017/05/19/arts/dance/on-the-frivolities-of-ballet-the-contradictory-art.html.
156. And why, after all this, a defense? I suppose I am tired of being asked to justify what I love. Maybe I want to offer a final answer, a response so decisive that it shuts the door on derision and contempt. *Perfume?* a colleague asked me recently when I described my collection, all

those scented boxes stored in the cool seclusion of a cabinet. We were making small talk before a faculty meeting, and I happened to mention a new bottle I had just purchased. I was trying to explain how seamlessly the jasmine slides into the tuberose. Like silk voile, I said. Like a pavlova, a great tutu of meringue topped with berries and whipped cream. I said that a well-made perfume can resemble a well-formed poem; great skill often renders itself invisible and, therefore, is easily dismissed, waved away as a vain performance. *Perfume?* my colleague repeated. I thought I heard judgment in his question. That single, interrogatory word—*Perfume?*—seemed to suggest I was as unserious as my passion, perhaps not a credible scholar in the end. And then we were being called into the conference room, summoned inside for a vote, a few hours governed by *Robert's Rules of Order*. What did it matter? It is almost impossible to persuade a colleague of anything while standing in a hallway, our faces greenish-yellow from the bureaucratic light. But, you, reader, have traveled with me all the way to the end of these endnotes. So, I'll confess: If I could give myself a name, it might not be scholar. It might be epicure or enthusiast. It might be lover instead.

Bibliography

Adams, Richard. *Watership Down*. 1972. Scribner, 2005.

Arnold, Rebecca. *Fashion: A Very Short Introduction*. Oxford University Press, 2009.

Aucoin, Matthew. *The Impossible Art: Adventures in Opera*. Farrar, Straus and Giroux, 2021.

Austen, Jane. *Emma*. Vol. 4 of *The Oxford Illustrated Jane Austen: Emma*. Oxford University Press, 1988.

——. *"Northanger Abbey" and "Persuasion."* Vol. 5 of *The Oxford Illustrated Jane Austen:* Oxford University Press, 1988.

——. *Pride and Prejudice*. Vol. 2 of *The Oxford Illustrated Jane Austen:* Oxford University Press, 1988.

Barquin, Juan. "On Barbie and Greta Gerwig's Colorful, Complicated Portrait of Humanity." *Autostraddle*, July 21, 2023. https://www.autostraddle.com/barbie-review.

Batchelor, David. *Chromophobia*. Reaktion Books, 2000.

Berger, John. *Ways of Seeing*. 1972. Penguin, 1990.

Broadway, Anna. "Pink Wasn't Always Girly." *The Atlantic*, August 12, 2013. www.theatlantic.com/sexes/archive/2013/08/pink-wasnt-always-girly/278535/.

Brombert, Victor. "Lessons of Montaigne." In *The Pensive Citadel*. University of Chicago Press, 2023.

Brown, Jericho. *The Tradition*. Copper Canyon Press, 2019.

BIBLIOGRAPHY

Calvino, Italo. *Six Memos for the Next Millenium*. Trans. Geoffrey Brock. Mariner Classics, 2016.

Carnevali, Barbara. *Social Appearances: A Philosophy of Display and Prestige*. Trans. Zakiya Hanafi. Columbia University Press, 2020.

Cavell, Stanley. *Pursuits of Happiness: The Hollywood Comedy of Remarriage*. Harvard University Press, 1981.

Danto, Arthur C. *What Art Is*. Yale University Press, 2014.

Dickinson, Emily. *The Poems of Emily Dickinson*. Ed. R. W. Franklin. Belknap Press, 1998.

Doty, Mark. *Dog Years: A Memoir*. HarperCollins, 2007.

Dubrow, Jehanne. *throughsmoke: an essay in notes*. New Rivers Press, 2019.

Eliot, George. *Middlemarch*. 1871–72. Penguin Classics, 2003.

Ephron, Nora. *I Feel Bad About My Neck*. Knopf, 2006.

——. *When Harry Met Sally*. Knopf, 1990.

Erens, Pamela. "It Can Be Embarrassing to Love Dorothea." *Paris Review*, August 8, 2013. https://www.theparisreview.org/blog/2013/08/08/it-can-be-embarrassing-to-love-dorothea/.

Evening ensemble. *Texas Fashion Collection*. University of North Texas. https://digital.library.unt.edu/ark:/67531/metadc1955546/?q=future%20of%20fashion.

OED Online. Oxford University Press. S.v., "exclamation point, n." Accessed September 2022. www-oed-com.libproxy.library.unt.edu/view/Entry/65814?redirectedFrom=exclamation+point#eid4963951.

Flaubert, Gustave. *Madame Bovary*. Trans. Geoffrey Wall. Penguin Classics, 1992.

Frederick, John T. "Hawthorne's 'Scribbling Women.'" *New England Quarterly*. June 1975. https://www.jstor.org/stable/364660?seq=1.

Friedman, Vanessa. "All Pinked Out." *New York Times*, July 24, 2023. www.nytimes.com/2023/07/24/style/all-pinked-out.html.

Goldberg, Emma. "Where Do We Stand on the Exclamation Point?" *New York Times*, September 27, 2019. https://www.nytimes.com/2019/09/27/style/exclamation-points.html.

Gopnick, Adam. "Voltaire's Garden." *New Yorker*, February 27, 2005. https://www.newyorker.com/magazine/2005/03/07/voltaires-garden.

Grimm, Jacob and Wilhem Grimm. *The Original Folk and Fairy Tales of the Brothers Grimm: The Complete First Edition*. Trans. Jack Zipes. Princeton University Press, 2014.

Hart, Maria Teresa. *Doll*. Bloomsbury Academic, 2022.

Hay, Carol. "Barbie Used to Be Everything Wrong with Patriarchal Beauty Ideals, Feminist Professor Says. Now She's Closer to 'Queer Camp.'" *Fortune Magazine*, July 17, 2023. https://fortune.com/2023/07/17/barbie-movie-beauty-standards-patriarchy-queer-camp-femmephobia-feminism-scholar.

Herdrich, Stephanie L. "Madame X." In *Fashioned by Sargent*, ed. Erica E. Hirshler et al. MFA Publications, 2023.

Hollander, John, ed. *American Wits: An Anthology of Light Verse*. Library of America, 2003.

——. *Rhyme's Reason: A Guide to English Verse*. Yale University Press, 2001.

Ibsen, Henrik. *A Doll's House and Other Plays*. Trans. Deborah Dawkin and Erik Skuggevik. Penguin Classics, 2016.

Indermaur, Katherine. *I/I*. Seneca Review Books, 2022.

James, Caryn. "It's Harry [Loves] Sally in a Romance of New Yorkers and Neuroses." *New York Times*, July 12, 1989. www.nytimes.com/1989/07/12/movies/review-film-it-s-harry-loves-sally-in-a-romance-of-new-yorkers-and-neuroses.html.

Lawrence, D. H. *D. H. Lawrence: Late Essays and Articles*. Ed. James T. Boulton. Cambridge University Press, 2014.

Macaulay, Alastair. "On the Frivolities of Ballet, the Contradictory Art." *New York Times*, May 19, 2017. www.nytimes.com/2017/05/19/arts/dance/on-the-frivolities-of-ballet-the-contradictory-art.html.

May, Katherine. *Wintering: The Power of Rest and Retreat in Difficult Times*. Riverhead Books, 2020.

Miller, Madeline. Introduction to *Watership Down* by Richard Adams. Scribner, 2005.

Montaigne, Michel. *The Complete Essays of Montaigne*. Trans. Donald M. Frame. Stanford University Press, 1965.

Newsome, W. Jake. *Pink Triangle Legacies: Coming Out in the Shadow of the Holocaust*. Cornell University Press, 2022.

Ngai, Sianne. *Our Aesthetic Categories: Zany, Cute, Interesting*. Harvard University Press, 2015.

O'Hara, Helen. "The Best Thing About the Barbie Movie? It's Going to Annoy All the Right People." *Stylist*, July 21, 2023. www.stylist.co.uk/entertainment/film/barbie-movie-feminist-backlash/805957.

Okrent, Arika. "The Listicle as a Literary Form." *University of Chicago Magazine*, January–February 2014. https://mag.uchicago.edu/arts-humanities/listicle-literary-form.

Orwell, George. *1984*. 1949. Signet Classic, 1961.

Parker, Dorothy. "Résumé." *American Wits: An Anthology of Light Verse*. Ed. John Hollander. Library of America, 2023.

Pascale, Blaise. *Pensées*. Trans. A. J. Krailsheimer. Penguin Classics, 1995.

Pollock, Griselda. "The Overlooked Radicalism of Impressionist Mary Cassatt." *Frieze*, September 18, 2003, www.frieze.com/article/overlooked-radicalism-impressionist-mary-cassatt.

Reza, Yasmina. "The Fabric of Life: An Interview with Yasmina Reza." Interview by Violane Huisman. *Paris Review*, February 20, 2015. www.theparisreview.org/blog/2015/02/20/the-fabric-of-a-life-an-interview-with-yasmina-reza.

——. *God of Carnage*. Trans. Christophere Hampton, Farrar, Straus and Giroux, 2008.

Roberts, Michèle. Preface to *Madame Bovary* by Gustave Flaubert. Penguin Classics, 1992.

Shaffer, Peter. *Amadeus*. 1972; Harper Perennial, 2001.

Shakespeare, William. *The Oxford Shakespeare: The Complete Works*, 2nd ed. Ed. Stanley Wells, Gary Taylor, John Jowett, and William Montgomery. Oxford University Press, 2005.

Shōnagon, Sei. *The Pillow Book*. Trans. Meredith McKinney. Penguin Classics, 2007.

Shteyngart, Gary. "The Rise of the Inflatable Chicken Resistance." *New York Times*, October 20, 2025. https://www.nytimes.com/2025/10/20/opinion/no-kings-protest-chicago-tactical-frivolity.html.

Snyder, Timothy. *On Tyranny: Twenty Lessons from the Twentieth Century*. Crown, 2017.

Sontag, Susan. *Against Interpretation: And Other Essays*. Picador, 1961.

Spector, Stephen. *The Quotable Guide to Punctuation*. Oxford University Press, 2017.

St. Claire, Kassia. *The Secret Lives of Color*. Penguin Books, 2017.

Stein, Gertrude. *Lectures in America*. Beacon Press, 1935.

Strunk, William, Jr., and E. B. White. *The Elements of Style*. 4th ed. Allyn & Bacon, 2000.

Ticknor, Caroline. *Hawthorne and His Publisher*. Kessinger, 2010.

Tolentino, Jia. "The Year that Skin Care Became a Coping Mechanism." *New Yorker*, December 18, 2017. www.newyorker.com/culture/cultural-comment/the-year-that-skin-care-became-a-coping-mechanism.

Veblen, Thorstein. *The Theory of the Leisure Class.* 1899; Oxford University Press, 2007.

Voltaire. *Candide, ou l'Optimisme.* 1759; Gallimard, 2003.

Weiner, Jonah. "Why Are Pants So Big (Again)?" *New York Times,* March 3, 2024. https://www.nytimes.com/2024/03/03/magazine/big-pants-style.html.

Wiland, Harry. "Q&A with Russian Jewish Writer Gary Shteyngart." *Jewish Journal,* September 7, 2006. https://jewishjournal.com/culture/arts/13641/.

Wilbur, Richard. *Collected Poems: 1943–2004.* Ecco, 2006.

Wilcox, Melissa M. *Queer Nuns: Religion, Activism, and Serious Parody.* New York University Press, 2018.

Wiley, Chris. "When Lee Miller Took a Bath in Hitler's Tub." *New Yorker,* January 9, 2024. https://www.newyorker.com/culture/photo-booth/when-lee-miller-took-a-bath-in-hitlers-tub.

Woods, Chavisa. "The Insidious Faux-Feminism of Barbie." *Full Stop,* August 7, 2023. www.full-stop.net/2023/08/07/features/essays/chavisa-woods/the-insidious-faux-feminism-of-barbie/?utm_source=substack&utm_medium=email.

Index

INDEX

INDEX

INDEX

Printed and bound by CPI Group (UK) Ltd, Croydon, CR0 4YY

17/08/2026

14943332-0001